An Unconventional Portrait of Yourself

AN UNCONVENTIONAL PORTRAIT

OF

YOURSELF

by

D. E. HARDING

The Shollond Trust

London

Published by The Shollond Trust

87B Cazenove Road

London N16 6BB

England

headexchange@gn.apc.org

www.headless.org

The Shollond Trust is a UK charity, reg. no 1059551

Design and conversion to print by rangsgraphics.com

ISBN 978-1-914316-37-1

CONTENTS

PREFACE

An Unconventional Portrait of Yourself was completed by Douglas Harding in 1941, so it shows his thinking about a year before he saw that he was headless. Challenging the conventional view of who you are, Douglas demonstrates how everything is within you, that you do not stop at the boundary of your skin but encompass the whole universe:

"When you hear music and the songs of birds, when you look at pictures and flowers and the faces of your friends, you can truly say: 'It is myself that I see and hear. I include all these; they are not outside me. Instead of being trapped in a little body, I am at large out there among these well-known and well-loved things.'"

Although Douglas was not yet seeing the headless space that is capacity for all things, he had worked out that this timeless, spaceless, all-encompassing identity is what we are.

This book radiates a deep appreciation of the miracle and mystery of life. Douglas implores you not to live your life without taking time to wonder about it:

"...on your death-bed it will be too late to start wondering what your life was about, and I, for one, would be sorry to die without ever having found time to be surprised at my living."

At the end of the book, Douglas sums up:

"...we have found that you are unlimited, unseparate, and un-knowable, and that a full realisation of these three facts can overcome your sense of restriction, your loneliness, and your unrest. A man who could always live in the knowledge that he spreads out to embrace the whole, that he is inextricably mixed up with every part of the whole, and that his entire being is sustained by the whole, would have peace, security, and happiness."

This book, written for younger readers, shows Douglas exercising his communication skills — he uses straight-forward, everyday language, with many simple — and amusing — drawings to illustrate his ideas. (Both his determination to write in a way that anyone could understand, and his use of drawings, found even greater scope in his next and greatest book, The Hierarchy of Hierarchy of Heaven and Earth. Many ideas in that book can be found, in embryonic form, in The Unconventional Portrait of Yourself.)

The essential message of this book, backed by deep and courageous thinking, and written with heart, with passion, is that you are not what convention says you are. You are far older, deeper, wiser, more mysterious. Don't let your life pass by without appreciating the miracle that is 'you'.

Richard Lang

INTRODUCTORY

In this book I am going to take it for granted that you are interested in yourself, in what you really are. I shall assume that you do not imagine the subject to be dull, dangerous, or wicked.

Of all things this subject of yourself is surely the most exciting and important — exciting, because you are like an unexplored country full of surprises at every turn, with half-glimpsed forbidden territories and hints of impenetrable mysteries just ahead of you; important, because your life is short and to take it for granted is to put aside your greatest possession without glancing at it. When someone sends you a present you lose no time in undoing the parcel and looking at the contents. You (body and mind and whatever else you may be) are more intriguing and valuable than any mere chattel. How could you fail to be interested?

What are you? That is the question which this book asks. The answers are surprising, but it must be admitted that they are also vague. In fact, one of the main conclusions we shall come to is that you don't know what you are, and you never can know. You are a gigantic question-mark. Common-sense of course, disagrees, and says you have a pretty good idea of what you amount to; it is aware of no special mystery; it is quite content with the superficial you. But common-sense is hopelessly inadequate, and in some respects its view is positively wrong. It ignores all but the surface, which it mistakes for the substance. Its world is largely unreal. You owe it to yourself to face up to the facts however disturbing they may prove, and, though the truth about yourself may be for the most part unknown and unknowable, an honest question-mark is better than an illusion. In any case, to search for the reality behind appearances is an absorbing occupation, carrying its own reward.

In the following pages, accuracy will often have to give way to simplicity of expression. Whenever I have to choose between the technical word and the ordinary word, I shall choose the ordinary one, and wherever I have an excuse for drawing something (whether it is really picturable or not) I shall draw it. If I can help by these means to make an idea live for you, to make it your own even though it becomes a little distorted in the process, then I shall achieve my object. I do not want to put you on distant nodding terms with a host of technicalities — in the world of ideas, as well as in life, a slightly disreputable friend is worth a dozen correct acquaintances.

CHAPTER I

THE PORTRAIT WITHOUT A SITTER

What are you?

Let us try to answer this question plainly and simply, dispensing with frills. Let us appeal to common-sense.

Common-sense says you are your body. The way you talk about yourself makes this evident. For example, if you have a pain in the stomach you say "I am ill." If a man hits you on the nose, you say "He hit me." When a man's body dies you say "He died." Even a philosopher says he has had a good meal, instead of telling you how well his body dined.

Obviously we look upon our bodies as ourselves. Common-sense says that, whatever else you may be, you are your body and your body is you.

What is your body?

According to common-sense it is a mass of flesh and bone weighing a hundred and fifty pounds or so, some five or six feet tall, and furnished with legs, arms, and so forth. The details of your inside can be left to your doctor — they are his business. As far as you are concerned, your body is what it seems to be. You know what it is.

Look at your hand. There it is out there, a solid object about a foot away from your eyes, a familiar sight with nothing very mysterious about it.

But let us consider the way you see your hand.

Light falls on your skin, and from there travels to your eye, where it hits the screen at the back of your eyeball and makes a picture of your hand. There is your hand inside your eyeball, tiny, flattened out and hanging upside down.

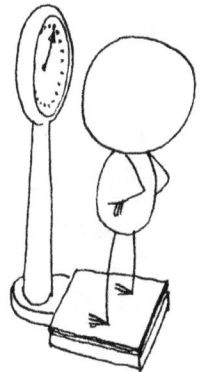

Though still recognisable, your hand is not what it was when it started out. But more drastic changes are yet to come. Seeing does not end with inverted pictures inside your eyes. The pictures have to be translated into a sort of code and telegraphed to your brain. And then your brain has to decipher the message and construct an entirely new kind of picture, a mental picture of your hand, apparently made solid again, pushed out of your head and a foot distant, enlarged to full size, and turned the right way up. When you make this mental picture you 'see your hand.'

No doubt none of this is new to you, especially if you are an amateur photographer. But have you realised that the well-known facts of sight make nonsense of common-sense? If you have, the world will never be quite the same place for you as it was before.

Let us go over the process of seeing, this time rather more carefully.

In the first place, we say that what links the hand out there with the hands inside your eyes is light. What is light? We are in the habit of thinking that because we have given something a name and observed some of its habits we understand what it is. Admittedly scientists have theories about the way in which light jumps from this place to that; they know how fast it travels, and under what circumstances it turns corners. But they cannot tell what light is. Or, if they can, they do so by explaining it in terms of some equally profound mystery like photons or ether waves.

What is it that goes on in the gap between the hand out there and the hand in your eyeball?

Something or other, it seems, must travel the gap, but that something or other certainly is not your hand, or even an image or picture of it. Whatever it is that makes the journey is apparently unlike what exists at the starting point and at the destination. It is as if your hand were to broadcast a detailed description of itself in Morse code which your eyes pick up, decipher, and use as directions for making a painting.

At school we drew diagrams to show how light behaves, and sup-posed we had explained something. The straight lines and arrows had a satisfying appearance, a look of finality. It never occurred to us that we could no more draw a diagram explaining how A-B got to B-A than we could draw a diagram explaining how pleased we were when the holidays came round.

But if we know next to nothing about the way in which informa-tion crosses the gap between your hand and your eye, and how the journey is accomplished, what guarantee have we that there are no mishaps en route? How do we know that the original message was correctly translated into code? How do we know that the message tells the whole story about your hand? How do we know that the pic-ture in your eye is not distorted in the making?

We know it is distorted — to the extent of being upside-down, flat and undersized. We have no guarantee it has not been distorted in many other ways.

Anyhow, there they are for what they are worth — the coloured portraits of your hand at the back of your eyes, and somehow your brain has got to get into touch with them.

How this is done is a mystery. Even the experts know almost noth-ing about how the immensely complicated details of the pictures in your eyes are turned into a sort of description or report, and how that report is sent off along the telegraph wires to your brain. To refer to electro-chemical changes in the nerve fibres (say) may be impres-sive — it is certainly not an explanation. Explanations which add to the mystery may be both interesting and important, but they are not explanations.

What happens on the way, though obscure enough, is almost com-prehensible compared with events at the terminus. There the brain picks up the code message sent out by the eye, gets busy, and builds an idea. The idea is of your hand, seemingly a foot away, right-side-up, and solid-looking.

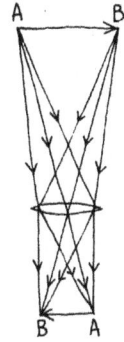

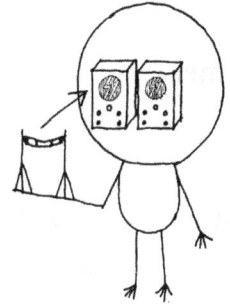

Something very odd indeed has happened. Up till now, events have been occurring in space — the original hand was about eight inches long and four inches broad; light travelled a foot from your hand to your eye; the picture in your eye was so many hundredths of an inch long; the connecting link of nerve fibres between your eye and your brain can be seen and measured; and, finally, the region of your brain which deals with seeing fills a definite number of cubic millimetres. All these things can be measured, but they lead to something that cannot be measured, because it does not occupy any space at all.

The mental picture you make of your hand is not inside your head. Nor, for that matter, is it outside your head, though I have drawn it that way in the diagram. The mental picture exists, but it is nowhere. It is not domiciled in space at all, and is no more inside your brain-pan than fifty miles away. (If you find it difficult to believe in a real thing which does not take up any room, I see no special harm in thinking of it as filling the entire universe, as situated at the same time in your head, on the dome of St. Paul's, and in the space between the stars — as, in fact, anywhere).

Since your mental picture of your hand is strictly speaking no-where, it can be neither big nor little. When you think of a grain of sand your thought is not small, any more than looking at elephants gives you a swelled head. Your mental picture of your hand is not eight inches long, though it is of such an object — which is not at all the same thing.

If by some miracle you were able to look inside your own eye at this moment, you would see the print of this page hanging upside-down, like a tiny poster stuck on the rear wall of your eyeball. But if, more miraculously still, you were able to vivisect your own brain, you would never find printing or page, or pictures of either, however long you looked for them. They are not there. The book and the hand of your experience are not something outside your body, neither are they something inside your eyes or your brain. They are mental things, objects which are nowhere, yet real.

Fantastic? Of course it is fantastic, and appears more so the more you think about it. Looking at your hand seems to be the simplest process in the world, but once you cease to take seeing for granted, and start on the most elementary investigation, you find miracles that make the cleverest saint in the Calendar look like an incompetent amateur. If you knew exactly how you see your hand you would probably know everything.

Our ignorance of the whole matter is profound. For instance, we have no idea to what extent, if any, your mental picture is like your hand out there — the original hand, so to speak. Can you think of the pinkness of the original hand getting itself put into code, flying invisibly through space to your eyeball, getting itself de-coded, and then put into code again along quite different lines, and finally advancing to your brain where it is used by some mysterious painter to help him to colour something which has no size and is nowhere in particular? It certainly sounds like the most arrant nonsense.

The truth is that you have a clear mental picture of your hand and its pinkness, and that is all you can be quite certain of. If you think you know what it is out there which corresponds to the pinkness of the hand you see, then you deceive yourself.

And that leads us to a bigger question. If the colour of your hand is a creation of your mind, what about its shape? What about its very existence?

You cannot be aware of things with your eyeballs, or with your brains, or with any other part of your body. You can only know with your mind, and seeing is one kind of knowing. All the things you see, from your hand to the Milky Way, are in your mind. They are mental pictures.

The size and shape and texture and colour of the things you see, and even their existence, are, for you, ideas. All the people and buildings and flowers and trees and stars you have ever laid eyes on have been pictures in your mind. How else could you have seen them?

It is unnecessary to go so far as to say that your hand and people and buildings, and so on, exist only in your mind. What we can say is that you have no means of finding out what these things are like in themselves, out there. Your mind can only appreciate what gets through to it (so to speak), and when you consider all the chopping and changing that goes on in the process of getting through, it is fairly certain you can have no notion of what is there at the start.

If this is the first time you have thought about such matters, you are probably undecided whether to look on these arguments as useless mystification or verbal trickery. You suspect a line of thought that ends up by undermining your whole world, making the 'real' seem unreal.

Suppose you are walking down the middle of the street, and a large, red, and dangerous tramcar is rushing towards you, making a great deal of noise. Do you gaze calmly upon the tramcar and say to yourself: "In the first place there is not just one tramcar. There are no fewer than four tramcars — the apparently solid one out there, two small ones, upside-down and flattened, within my eyes, and another in my mind which belongs to a different sort of world altogether and is nowhere — and of these four the last is the only real one for me"? You do not. You get out of the way as fast as you can. If you stayed to investigate the first tramcar's reality or unreality, you would get an unpleasantly vivid demonstration — but of what, exactly?

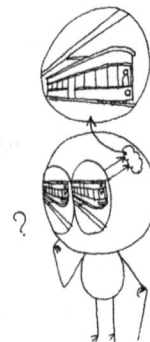

You would probably get killed, of course. But would this fact prove that, as far as you are concerned, the tramcar is not a mental tramcar? It would not. Your pain as the tramcar hit you, would, like all pain, be a mental experience. Your injuries, as you looked upon them and thought about them, would be present in your mind. And your death would be a mental switching-off, or at any rate a change of some sort in your mind. The incident would have demonstrated, not that the tramcar was not a mental picture, but that the vivid idea of a tramcar descending upon you, when followed by the vivid idea of your not getting out of the way, leads up to the all-too-vivid idea of pain and finally to a switching-off of all ideas. The whole series of events is mental.

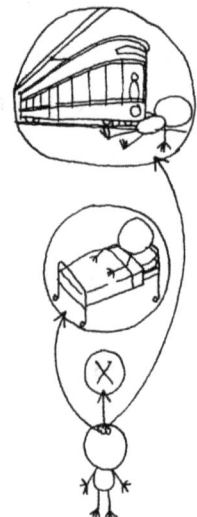

You know that this unpleasant mental sequence is more or less inevitable unless you change it by introducing the vivid idea of dodging the tramcar. And that is what you do.

Supposing we admit that seeing is by itself an unreliable guide to what exists out there one foot in front of you, are there not other clues, other channels by which information may be received? When you snap your fingers you hear the sound they make; with one hand you can feel the shape of the other; if you were eaten by a tiger, your hand would have, for the tiger, both taste and smell. Is not the evidence of all the senses, when taken together, sufficient to establish what your hand is really like?

What happens when you hear your fingers snap?

Waves are set up, which travel through the air to your ear where they beat against your ear-drum and make it vibrate. The vibrations are at once transmitted to a vessel that is like a tiny piano full of liquid. When the liquid is set in motion some of the 'piano wires' (there are about 10,000 of them) vibrate in sympathy, and a message saying which wires are vibrating is telegraphed to your brain. The result is that you 'hear a sound.'

Where is this sound that you hear? It is not in your fingers; it is not in the air that bridges the gap between your fingers and your ear; it is not in the vessel behind your ear-drum nor in the piano wires; it is not in the message that travels from the piano wires to your brain; and, finally, it is not in your brain. It is 'in' your mind. The outside world, and all the immensely complicated events in your head, are silent. It is your mind that provides the sound.

Similarly with feeling, smell and taste. They are mental things. No doubt something in the 'outside' world has given rise to them, but whatever that something is, it is certainly nothing like your sensations.

It is your idea of your hand which you know, which is vividly real to you as a shape, as a patch of colour, as a thing which can be felt and heard. The hand out there, the thing as it actually is in itself, you cannot know.

And the same is true of your entire body. Common-sense thinks it knows what your body is, but it is mistaken. What you call your body is an idea, or rather an extremely elaborate system of ideas, in your mind. If the hundred and fifty pounds of flesh and bone can be said to have any kind of existence on its own account, apart from your mind and mine, the nature of that existence is entirely hidden from us.

It follows that when common-sense says you are your body as it exists out there in itself, common-sense is really saying that you are unknown and unknowable.

CHAPTER II

THE WALKING CITY

We set out to paint a portrait of you — but the sitter vanished.

"Which," adds common-sense, "does not get one very far… After all, every man behaves as if he knows what he is and what the world around him is like. And, though these assumptions may be unjustified, they seem to work. If this 'idea' we have of our bodies is good enough for men in general and for scientists in particular (and scientists ought to know) it is good enough for me. Philosophy leads nowhere, whereas common-sense, and science which is only common-sense developed, accepts the world we know, and, having done so, goes a long way towards explaining it. If you want to know what you are, ask the scientist, not the philosopher."

Let us then, for the moment, ignore the conclusions of the previous chapter, and again ask the question: What are you?

Common-sense replies that you are one body, endowed with one life, an individual.

How does this life arise? From what does this individuality spring? What is the basis of your existence as the man you are?

If we try to answer these questions by examining your bodily structure, can we, by careful searching, strip you of non-essentials and find somewhere the real you, the core and centre of your being? However long we search we can find no such thing. We find only — a vast animal population.

These millions and billions of animals are not intruders, or casual inhabitants, or even paying guests — they are you. You are, in fact, a walking city.

The citizens, which are called cells, are of many shapes and sizes, each being fitted for the work he does. Some of them move around your body taking nourishment by the way and behaving almost as

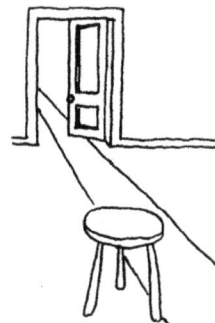

though they were loose in a pond. Others — they are in the majority — lead a sedentary life and sit at home getting on with their jobs and having their food brought to them.

Just as a town's life can only go on properly if its citizens make bread, and attend to the drains and the roads, and repair old buildings and put up new ones, so do you live only if your millions of citizens do their jobs conscientiously. They little realise, of course, that by scavenging, and operating telephones (so to speak), and doing building work, and fetching and carrying, and bearing children, they make you possible, that they are you. When a police-cell, creeping through your flesh, arrests and devours a trespasser, he is not interested in you or your health; he is interested in getting his food. All the same, his unawareness, and the unawareness of his fellow-citizens, does not affect their efficiency.

Picture to yourself what happens when you stretch out your hand to open a page of this book. There is great municipal activity, and it is beautifully organised. Millions of citizens get busy: overseers give instructions, telephone operators put through trunk-calls, information bureaux get out reports, brawny workmen push and pull. Result: your arm moves.

What you do, your cells do. Your life is built out of their life.

If a pair of them were clever enough to think and talk, this is what they might say:

1st Cell: (A genius amongst cells) Why do we work so hard scavenging, operating telephones, having families, building this and that, or whatever it is we so earnestly do?

2nd Cell: To earn our livings, of course. A cell must work for his dinner.

1st Cell: Yes I know that. But I was wondering… Don't you think it is possible that there is something else in the world, a sort of god-cell — call him Jack Robinson — who is somehow responsible for all this feverish activity?

2nd Cell: Where is this Jack Robinson? I'll believe in him when I see him.

1st Cell: I haven't seen him either, yet I have a feeling… Perhaps he isn't out there, but here. I mean, in you and me. It's contrary to common-sense I know. All the same –

2nd Cell: That sounds dangerously like mysticism.

1st Cell: I have it! We — you and I and our fellow-cells — are this Jack Robson. When we do our little job of work we do his big job of work. Our little bodies are his big body. Our little lives are his big life. I admit that only in moments of insight does the idea really mean something to me. Nevertheless it is true.

Just as your supernaturally intelligent cell finds it difficult to grasp the idea that his life is a bit of your life, so, perhaps, do you find it difficult to grasp the idea that you are a walking metropolis, of which he is a citizen. When a police-cell in your blood is about to devour a criminal he does not preface his meal with any pious remarks about your welfare. And in much the same way you, when faced with the on-coming tramcar, do not say to yourself: "We — all the millions of us — must co-operate and do something about this. Get busy, cells!" You and your cells are sublimely indifferent to one another. Unaware, you just carry on in your different spheres.

The question now arises: how do you, one and indivisible, intelligent, self-conscious, arise from these multitudes of amazingly efficient, yet minute, stupid, un-self-conscious animals? If a million human idiots cannot between them muster a single intelligent thought, how is it that you, who are a walking asylum of brainless and blind deaf-mutes, are also a creature whose field of thought is the universe?

Nobody knows how it happens. We can and we do give high-sounding names to the mystery, and multiply instances of it, and probe its surface a little, only to find more and more mystery underneath.

One view is that the qualities which make you a human being are hidden all the time in the animals of which you are composed. Another is that God did a sort of sleight-of-hand trick and slipped these qualities in while creation was looking in the other direction. A third opinion is that your human life and self-consciousness arise from

the extremely complicated personal relationships (as it were) of your animal population. Possibly there is something in all three 'explanations'. Possibly; but in reality they no more explain the situation than arrows in a diagram explain light.

You are like a sum that is always coming out wrong. A conjurer-mathematician takes the inhabitants of the walking city one by one, reckons them up, and gets X for an answer. Then he shuffles them, and having, after endless experiments, arranged them in extremely intricate patterns, he counts them again. This time they come to X + Y. No amount of checking and counter-checking can isolate or explain the intruder, and neither common-sense nor science can say exactly what it is or how it got there.

CHAPTER III

THE ART OF AMPUTATION

"All right," common-sense replies, "I know nothing about my body's interior, but this I do know: whatever may or may not go on within this hundred and fifty pounds of flesh and bone, however extraordinary this walking city may be, at least the city has walls. I know where I stop. My skin contains my body. The world is divided into two distinct parts — my body, and everything outside my body. Perhaps that fact is not very profound, but at least there is something definite about it.

"It is of no use," common-sense goes on, "pointing out that the distinction between me and the outside world is blurred because my mind is full of stars, tramcars, and all that I see. I am referring to myself as a body, which no tramcar or star has ever got mixed up with. I may be a skinful of mystery and the world may be an extraordinary place as well, but I do know where the one ends and the other begins. Only a sophist could argue otherwise."

Let us take up common-sense's challenge, and put a few questions.

Q. I see you have a set of false teeth. Are they a part of your body?

A. Of course not.

Q. Why not?

A. Because they are dead.

Q. But your bones are largely made of dead material deposited by living cells. Does it follow that your bones are not part of your body?

A. No. My bones are part of me because they are not loose and removable like my false teeth.

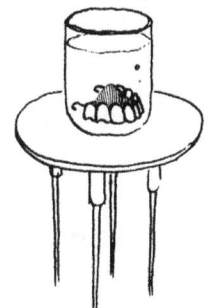

Q. Then a dead thing can be part of your body but a loose thing cannot be?

A. Correct.

Q. What about your gastric juice and your saliva? They are loose as well as dead. Are they part of your body?

A. I suppose they are.

Q. Then the looseness of your false teeth does not disqualify them for membership any more than their deadness disqualifies them. You will have to find another reason for excluding your dentures.

A. My false teeth are not part of my body, because they did not grow along with the rest of me.

Q. Please drink this glass of water. Now in a little while some of the water will be flowing in your arteries, and some of it will be inside certain of your cells. Will it then be part of you?

A. Yes.

Q. But the water did not grow up along with the rest of you. How, then, can it be part of you?

A. It does a useful job of work in connection with my body.

Q. That is the real reason why it is part of you?

A. Yes.

Q. And anything which does a useful job in connection with your body is part of it?

A. I suppose so.

Q. Then your false teeth are part of you!

Common-sense, however, feels it has been tricked. It is not satisfied, and demands further explanation.

Your body is a collection of tools and instruments. Your hand, for instance, is a tool for grasping things; your eyes are seeing-instruments; your legs are propellers. You, as a body, know how to grow these devices, which enable you to get to grips with the world.

But the natural tools you grow are hopelessly inadequate for the sort of life you lead. Your bare hand cannot write a letter, or cut up a piece of paper neatly, or bore a hole in a piece of wood. Your eye is a

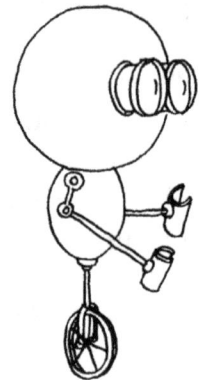

marvellous optical instrument, but it cannot register animals much smaller than a cheese-mite, or the details of the moon's surface. Your legs, however muscular, are inadequate when it comes to really fast travelling. Before you can do these things you have to grow. And this is precisely what you do — artificially.

You extend your body. To write a letter you grip a pen, and add that pen to your body. Temporarily, you have grown a nib at the end of your right arm. When you want to look at the details of a fly's leg, you grow, for the time being, a new front to your eyeball, in the form of a microscope. If you want to get somewhere quickly you grow wheels. When you want to break things you grow a hard fist, known as a hammer, for that purpose.

If you feel cold you grow a thick skin by putting on an overcoat, and as soon as you feel hot you slough it. When your natural teeth get beyond repair you grow an artificial set.

In fact, your body has two parts — the fleshly part that you are committed to for life, and the acquired part which you grow and un-grow as you please. The organs of the first body you take around with you always; the organs of the second you leave lying about, ready to be attached when you need them. Let us glance at some of this artificial anatomy of yours…

Take as an example a chair. When you sit on it you grow four more legs, making six in all, which is as many as a fly has. It is obviously convenient to have these four extra legs, yet be able to amputate them at will.

You can get up and leave four legs behind; a fly, on the other hand, has to take all its six legs round all the time, though they are as useless when the fly is on the wing as chair-legs are to you when you are walking.

Or take a pair of pincers. When you want to nip something, you pick up the pincers and grow a claw at the end of your arm. A lobster has done the same thing, but its claw, being natural, is a fixture. The lobster having rashly committed itself for life to nipping, has become incapable of boring, cutting, or scraping, whereas you are sensible

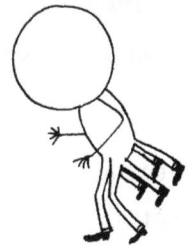

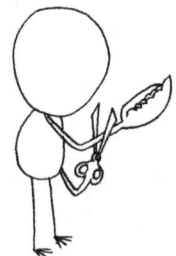

enough to grow an artificial claw that you can amputate at a moment's notice and grow again as gimlet, or a knife, or a razor, or a hundred other limb-endings.

At meal-times it would be useful if one of the finger-nails on your right hand were big enough and strong enough to function as a spoon, and one on the left hand could do service as a fork. But such protuberances would be in the way between meals. You find it much more convenient to have a set of metal finger-nails (so to speak) beside your plate, enabling you to grow a suitable pair of hands for dealing with each course.

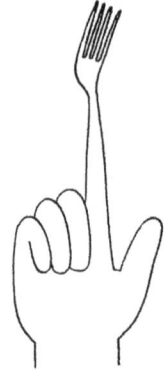

Modern sanitary practice demands that you shall eliminate your waste matter at the town's sewage farm, or in the sea. There are three conceivable ways of doing this. You might travel there daily. You (or nature for you) might grow a natural bowel between your house and the sewage works, presumably burying most of it beneath the pavements. Or you might grow an artificial bowel (known as a drain) of the same length, which you can amputate and re-grow as often as you wish. The superior efficiency of the third method is obvious.

If you want to hear your friend talking at the other end of the town, you may visit him; you may sit at home and grow a face so lopsided that your ear is up against his window (nature has done more extraordinary things than this before now); or you may grow an outer ear made of steel and bakelite and copper, and hang one end of it permanently in his flat and the other end in yours, with the middle part propped up on telegraph poles. Sensibly, you adopt the third method, and use an artificial ear that you can grow and un-grow many times an hour.

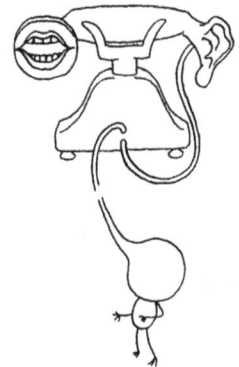

There are hardly any limits to this kind of growth. You are a monster that can develop, at a moment's notice, and in all directions, a body suitable for any occasion. When you want to broadcast your ideas you can grow a million mouths to shout with. When walking does not serve your purpose you can grow wings to fly with. When necessity arises, you can make yourself into a passable imitation of a fish, by growing an elaborate submarine body.

18

Suppose you are now eating a piece of toast. Actually, you started eating it weeks or months ago, when the wheat of which the bread was made was still standing in the field. Like any other herbivorous animal you grazed in that field, when your mechanical jaws (they are called harvesting-machines) bit off the corn stalks. Having eaten, you started digesting your food — the useless stalks and husks were removed in your first stomach, which is known as a threshing-machine. Your second stomach was the mill where the grain was ground into flour; the third, the bakery where the flour was made into bread; the fourth, the kitchen where the bread was toasted. By the time the toast arrives on your table it has already passed through four of your artificial stomachs, each of which has brought the raw material one stage nearer to its semi-final form, which is masticated toast lying inside your fifth stomach. Lastly, your personal digestive organs extract what is useful, while the rest is passed into your artificial bowel and returned to the land. Like a cow, you graze on the land and excrete on the land. The difference is that your body is several million times bigger than a cow's and capable of grazing in many fields at the same time, while excreting miles away.

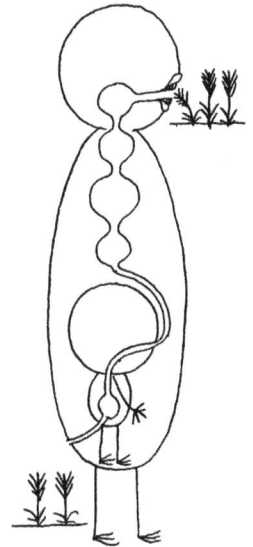

But even a cow is part of you. Her mouth as she grazes is your mouth; her teeth as she chews the cud are your teeth; her organs as she makes milk of the grass are your organs. You and I and all who drink milk are grass-eaters who have grown preliminary stomachs that are capable of dealing with such food.

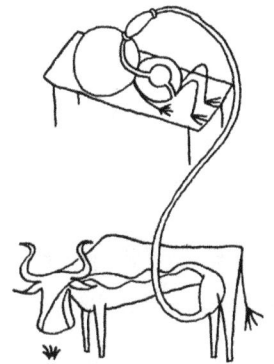

Everywhere you have mouths. When a fishing-net is dragged along the sea-bed it is your mouth feeding. When the sole that is about to be caught in the net has a meal, you have a meal. When the turkey you plan to kill for your Christmas dinner pecks corn in the farmyard, it is you who peck corn.

Everywhere you have eyes. When events in China or Peru are filmed and you see them on the cinema screen, the movie-cameras that shot the film are your eyes. A newspaper photographer is a man who walks around with another of your eyes in a leather case slung over his shoulder, and if he comes across something he thinks you would like to see, out comes your eye and up goes your eyelid.

Everywhere you have hands, from the tiniest tool to an industrial plant covering several square miles. A steam-hammer weighing a ton is just as truly an extension of your hand as the hammer in your home-carpentry set is, the only important distinction being that the steam-hammer is an energetic fist, so to speak, whereas the carpenter's hammer is not. A mechanical excavator scooping out the side of a mountain is a sort of energised spade, and a spade is not a mere spade, but a flat-shaped growth on the human arm, capable of easy amputation.

By far the greater part of your external eyes, and mouths, and stomachs, and hands, need men to work them. The men who operate steam-shovels, drive harvesters, bake bread, shoot films, milk cows, stoke locomotives, build houses, administer laws, clean drains — in fact, all men who do socially useful work — are as much your organs as are the devices they operate.

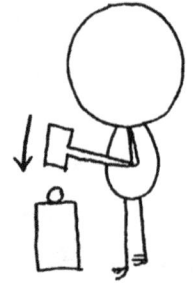

Tools, machines, animals, men — all things that help to make your life what it is — are extensions of your body. They are your means of life, in the same way that your hands and feet and liver are your means of life. In fact, many of your external or artificial organs are more important to you than a good deal of your body of flesh and blood. If you were deprived of your appendix and your fingernails and your eyebrows and even a part of your stomach, you would still be able to live the sort of life you do now, but the permanent amputation of a few of your preliminary stomachs, or your bowel extensions, or your shell, would leave you ill-equipped for life. It is quite possible you would not survive the operation. Whatever common-sense may say to the contrary, the jacket you are now wearing is, in a very real sense, at least as much a part of you as are your eyebrows.

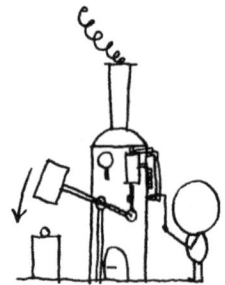

But where do you end?

If telephones are extensions of your ears and vocal chords, and food-factories and cattle are your stomachs, and trains, cars, aeroplanes and ships are your artificial legs and wings and fins, and libraries are your organs of memory, — if all these and much more are part of your greater body, where does this body stop and the outside world start?

If the cow that extracts nutriment from grass on your behalf is part of you, is not the grass that extracts nutriment from earth and air just as much part of you? The grass is as essential an item in the process of buttering your toast as the cow is and the milkmaid is. Grass, like the false teeth at the beginning of this chapter, does a useful job in connection with your body. It is part of you. And if it is part of you, are not the earth and the air, from which your nutriment ultimately comes, also part of you?

Similarly, if your house is your shell — a sort of hard loose skin from which your various artificial organs protrude — and this shell has to have a base which is the earth, is not the earth a necessary part of your shell and therefore part of you?

And so on. Your fleshly body shades off into your extended body, and both your fleshly and your extended body shade off into earth and air.

One way of summing up the situation is to say that the things which only you are dependent upon belong to your body in a special way, and the things which you and other people are dependent upon belong to your body in a remoter sense. The world is not divided into two parts — the part that is inside you, and the part that is outside you. All of it belongs to you, but in a greater or lesser degree.

You are like a sort of onion consisting of a core enveloped in five skins or layers, which, though distinguishable, are not sharply divided from one another. The core is your flesh — the mysterious walking city of the previous chapter. It is you in a special sense; you cannot change it for another one, nor can you share it with other people.

1. The first layer is the personal section of your artificial body — your clothes, spectacles, false teeth, fountain-pen, tooth-brush, and other articles which are for your use alone. This part of your body can undergo piecemeal amputation and replacement, and most of it could be grafted on to somebody else quite easily. All the same, you do not normally share this set of organs with other people; of all the vast anatomy of your artificial body it is the part which is most intimately your own.

2. The second layer is a world-wide organisation of domestic animals and plants, machines, books, roads, railways, ships, aeroplanes, buildings, and the men and women who make and work them. These are your body; you are dependent on them; they make your life human. But you share them with many other men, and in that sense they are less yours than your toothbrush and your kidneys are.

3. The third layer — the planet itself — is vaster still, and everybody's property. You are as dependent on this outer husk of yourself as you are on the flesh and blood at the centre, and it is only because you share the Earth with all other men, animals and plants, that we must describe it as an outlying portion of your anatomy. In a sense, of course, this third skin penetrates right to the core — your flesh is made up of earth and air; earth and air in various forms flow through your fleshly body in a constant stream, gradually replacing it and enabling it to live. Nobody can say where the earth and air of your fleshly body stop, and the earth and air of your food and drink and breath begin. And for good reason: your greater body is the Earth.

4. Why not the Sun also? In the Sun you have an organ yielding light, warmth, seasons, and the rhythm of day and night. The Sun, like the Earth and tramcars and your waist-coat and your heart, belongs to your body, and you would stand as much chance of survival if it were amputated as if a surgeon cut your brain out. The Sun, and its planet the Earth, are the material basis of your life. It takes them to keep you going.

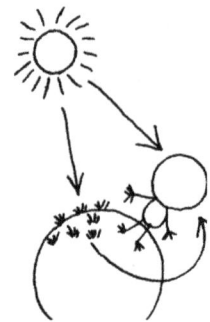

5. And finally there is the Universe itself, of which our Solar System is a mere particle. The Sun needs the Universe as its home; the Earth needs the Sun to light and warm it; the grass needs the Earth to grow on; the cow needs the grass to eat; your stomach needs the cow to keep it supplied with milk; the rest of your natural organs need your stomach to feed them. All are organs of your life, from the Universe to the least of your cell-citizens. In the last resort your body is the whole of things.

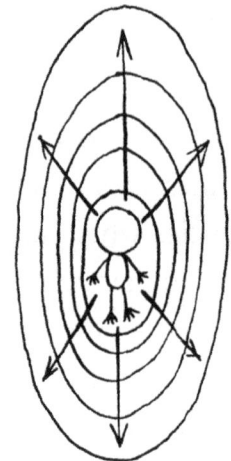

"This," says common-sense, "is the height of absurdity. I can follow you when you say that every time I use a pair of nut-crackers I grow a lobster-claw. You ask much when you tell me to look upon a herd of cows as so many detached stomachs of mine strolling in a meadow. You ask more when you tell me to look on this planet as my body. But when you tell me that I am the Universe you go too far. I am not specially humble, and I might be persuaded to regard myself as Creation's masterpiece, but I do draw the line at regarding myself as Creation."

Common-sense said that you are your body. We did not attempt to criticise this statement, so much as to see where it led us. It has led us to a view of yourself as spreading out till you embrace the Universe.

Whatever common-sense may say to the contrary, your body does not stop at your skin; you are not merely a hundred and fifty pounds of flesh hanging by the soles of your feet from a ball that is tearing through Space; the world is not something alien, apart from yourself. Your life is not here only, in your fleshly body, but in your greater body also — in tramcars and fields and cattle and houses and earth and air and sun. When you look at these you are looking at yourself.

At your centre lie the cells, with their huge question marks about matter, and life, and consciousness. At your extremities there lies the Universe with its even huger question-marks, and it is only a tiny fraction of what lies in between that common-sense can even start to understand.

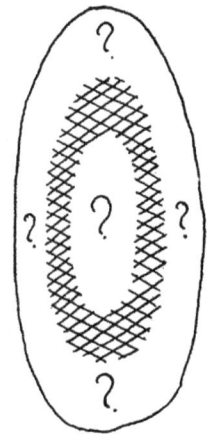

CHAPTER IV

THE CREEPER

"The error of this view," says common-sense, "is that it is too self-centred. You seem to look upon the Universe as a sort of service-flat, with all the latest labour-saving devices installed for your especial benefit. It is nothing of the kind — as you would quickly find out if you were to look at yourself from the outside. Get right away from yourself. Stand back and see your human life for what it is: one of two thousand million separate little human lives wresting a living out of an unfriendly world as best they can. Get a sane, common-sense angle on the human race, such as a complete outsider might get if he were up in the sky and looking at the earth through a powerful telescope."

Why not? There are as many ways of observing man as there are observers, and no doubt each way has something in it. The celestial observer's way ought to be as true as any other.

Our observer in the sky, then, is examining this planet, and he has no preconceived notions about what is happening on its surface. His telescope, incidentally, is not powerful enough for him to be able to see you and me. What is it he does see?

He sees the continents, of course, as islands in the oceans. He sees white poles, the yellowish patches of the Earth's deserts, and the green patches where the Earth is fertile. The coloured patches puzzle him. He notices that they expand and contract, as deserts and jungles, and land and sea, encroach on one another. He notices, too, that the green patches have a tendency to turn brown at regular intervals of time. He wonders what colours the patches.

But the piebald patterns have been present for so many millions of years that our observer has had time to get over his first surprise. What does amaze him is a more recent phenomenon. He cannot make up his mind whether it is a kind of gigantic creeper, an overgrown octopus, or a species of fungus. Whatever its nature, it seems to consist of

a vast network of extremely fine stalks or suckers. The stalks twist and turn over the Earth's surface, pushing their way round mountains and over rivers, and even (although our observer cannot see this) under the sea. At varying intervals they intersect, grow together in thick masses of different sizes, or dwindle away. In some places the stalks grow very slowly, or not at all. Elsewhere they flourish exceedingly.

Our observer is fascinated by the phenomenon that he has discovered, and he begins to take notes about its habits. He feels that such an extraordinary Plant (if it is a plant) deserves a Botany.

He notes, for example, that the Creeper seems to grow fastest midway between the Earth's poles and the equator. Though it has spread over the greater part of the land surface of the Earth, it evidently has a preference for a temperate climate. Rivers seem to attract it. The white poles, and to a less extent the permanently yellowish patches, it avoids.

A peculiar feature of the Creeper is the erratic rate of its growth. For many thousands of years it grew slowly and sporadically and there was much local withering, while every so often a sort of winter seemed to set in which depressed its life and caused large parts of it to die off. The Creeper survived, however, flourishing here and falling off there, but not achieving anything spectacular. Then, about a hundred years ago, it suddenly started to grow as it had never grown before. New, stout, healthy stalks — millions of them — thrust their way over hitherto untouched parts of the Earth's crust, burrowed under mountains when it was inconvenient to creep over them, threw branches over wide rivers, grew thousands of new stalk-masses, and greatly enlarged many of the old ones. For some unaccountable reason the Creeper had gained tremendous vitality. Its branches positively rushed about the Earth.

Of late, says our observer, there has been a distinct falling-off in vitality. Some sections of the Creeper seem to be suffering from a wasting disease. Or a winter, perhaps, is about to set in.

With a view to increasing his knowledge of the Creeper's natural history, our observer acquired a slightly more powerful telescope. Further discoveries follow:

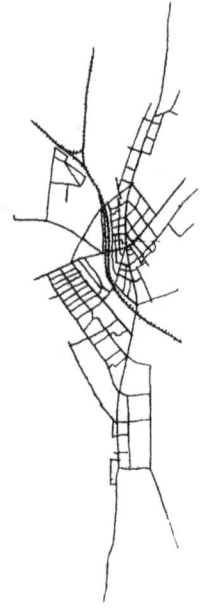

He finds out two ways in which the Creeper feeds. It feeds on the green patches of the Earth's surface — he can see a network of tiny surface suckers which apparently draw off nutriment. And it feeds by driving roots into the earth — roots which extract a black substance that seemingly acts as a powerful energiser. Perhaps he discovers how the Creeper drinks — by sending roots down to water, as well as by sucking up water from rivers and lakes.

He is able to see what looks like sap flowing in the Creeper's stalks — flowing most profusely during the daytime and where the stalks cluster thickest. But he cannot discover the nature of the sap: his telescope fails him. Unable to observe anything more of interest, he starts to make theories to account for the Creeper's habits.

At this stage he is visited by a common-sense human being. The following conversation takes place:-

O. Look at this extraordinary Creeper I have discovered — I call it a creeper, but I suspect it is as much animal as vegetable. More probably it is neither, but a third sort of living creature.

C.S. That is not a living creature. What you call stalks are merely railway lines and roads, and the buildings that line them. What you call stalk-clusters are nothing but cities and villages, as they are seen from an aeroplane. The objects you call roots are simply coal mines and iron mines and wells. The moving stuff you mistake for the sap is a stream of railway trains, lorries, cars, trams, and other vehicles. In short, everything you can see from here is absolutely dead.

O. Dead? How can an object that grows stalks and roots, and eats and drinks and suffers from diseases, and whose activity is increased by sunlight and diminished by darkness, be dead?

C.S. Tramcars and railway lines and roads and coal mines are just pieces of metal and earth. How can they be alive?

O. I don't know what you mean by tramcars and the other things you mention. I have never seen any. What I can see is the Creeper, which is as alive as you are. Surely that is evident.

C.S. On the contrary, it is a fallacy. I know what I am talking about, because I have seen these lorries and trains and trams, and ridden in

them, and watched them being made. Up here, you are too far away to know what is happening on Earth.

O. This is really most extraordinary. You say you live on the Earth, and yet you are unaware of the Creeper's life. Surely it is the most obvious thing about the planet… In any case, how do you distinguish a live thing from a dead one?

C.S. Living things grow, and feed, and eliminate, and suffer from diseases. The seasons affect them.

O. All that applies to the Creeper.

C.S. Now I come to think of it, there are deluded people who hold the theory that Society is a sort of god, or super-organism — a pernicious theory, invented by politicians of the worst kind and their friends. I am a democrat, and I believe in the responsibility of the individual man.

O. I am not talking about Society, but about the Creeper. You call its life a theory? Forget your earthly prejudices and look at the thing from here. There it is, growing and withering, eating and drinking, catching diseases and getting better again, before your very eyes. Why don't you call a tree a pernicious theory? Or yourself, for that matter?

C.S. You miss the point, which is that every bit of the tree is alive, whereas this so-called Creeper is mostly made up of dead pieces like tramcars.

O. I do not pretend to know anything about the Creeper's physiology, but I will take your word for it that many of its particles, considered separately, are dead. You are quite mistaken, however, when you say that a tree's particles are alive. They are not.

C.S. I suppose you refer to the molecules of which, according to chemists, the tree is built up. You seem to forget that molecules are extremely tiny, whereas tramcars are big things.

O. Do you mean to say that the Creeper fails to qualify as a living creature because it contains dead particles that are big, while the fact that a tree is made of tiny dead particles does not prevent it from being alive?

C.S. Er — yes.

O. But how absurd! You are misled by the fact that the Creeper has a coarser texture (so to speak) than the tree, though a coarse texture is just what one might expect in a creature that is millions of times more bulky than the biggest tree. It is easy to see the source of your stupidity: it is your size. On Earth you are big enough to see trees and tramcars but too small to see the Creeper. If you were tinier still — say about the size of a large molecule — you would not see even the tree. You would only see a collection of dead particles, and the tree would be to you nothing but a theory — probably a pernicious one. You would not be able to see the tree for the molecules, just as now you cannot see the Creeper for the tramcars.

Common-sense could not have done worse for itself than appeal for support to our celestial observer. Instead of getting the common-sense view confirmed, it has presented you with a picture of yourself as a particle in the body of a gigantic living creature.

This living creature is neither a gigantic creeper, nor an animal with sedentary habits, nor an overgrown Man, nor an Earth-bound god. It is not Society or Community, for it includes roads, cows, telephones, tramcars, sewers, and coal mines. Calling the Creeper Man gives the impression that it is human, and would be as perverse as calling you Nerve, or Brain Cell. Men-plus-their-artificial-organs would be a rather more accurate name. For the sake of brevity let us agree to call it the Earth-creature.

What kind of living thing, precisely, is the Earth-creature?

In the last chapter we found that your body does not stop at your skin but extends, by means of external organs such as telephones and drains and railways, over the Earth's surface. In that chapter you filled the picture. The time has come for us to shift our viewpoint to include the rest of humanity.

We have already seen that your external organs are not yours alone; you share them with other men. If you and I happen to share the same house, we are artificial Siamese twins who have a single external bowel, a single set of preliminary stomachs, a single shell, and a single system of extended ears, between the two of us.

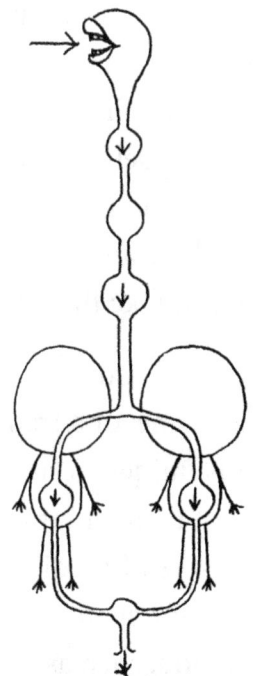

But the sharing of external organs does not stop with you and me. We possess a common body with our fellow-townsmen. The body has, amongst other organs, an alimentary canal system, which may be crudely represented thus:

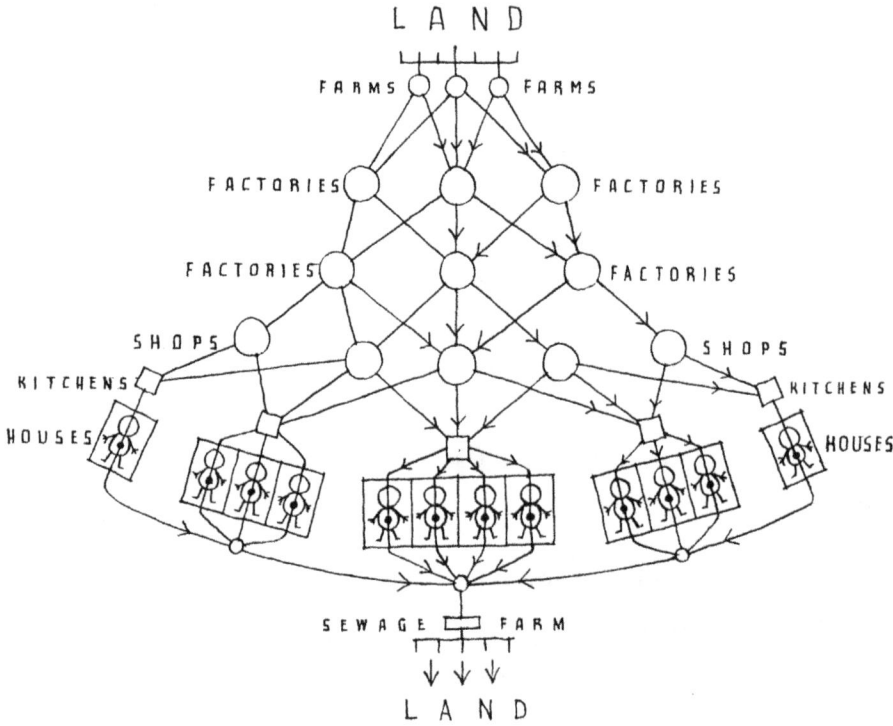

It is unnecessary to make diagrams to represent other parts of this great body. The creature's anatomy and physiology are familiar in detail — it is the fact of its existence as a single being, as alive and as actual as yourself, that is difficult to realise. To appreciate the reality of this gigantic individual, whose amazingly complex body consists of you and me and the rest of men, and of man's material works, it is necessary to take the celestial observer's point of view.

Once we do this, it is easy to see that the Earth-creature is nothing like you, or me, or a tramcar, or a railway line, built on an enormous scale. It is unique. It has its own diseases, which are quite unlike the diseases of men and tramcars and railway lines, and require a totally different sort of medicine. It has its own manner of growth, which is not like the manner of our growth, or a tramcar's. It has its own kinds of food, such as coal, iron ore, clay, timber-forests, cotton, and

mineral oil, in addition to the sort of food we eat. Its digestive organs, though they include ours, are of a totally different pattern. It has no heart, or brain, or blood, or hands, as we know them.

In our everyday jobs we help to maintain the Earth-creature's life. We are not called upon to supply it with physical energy (nowadays most of that is derived from its principal foods — coal and oil) so much as to see that its energy is used in self-maintenance and growth, instead of running to waste. Human intelligence is the knack by which the Earth-creature is able to regulate its vital processes, recover from diseases, and produce new organs when they are needed.

Let us take an example. When the Earth-creature is about to grow a new town it needs body-building food — trees, coal, iron ore, brick-earth, sand, clay, limestone. Accordingly, it devours enormous quantities of these foods, using saws and pneumatic drills and spades for teeth. The raw food is then passed into such digestive organs as workshops, mills, and kilns, which eventually turn out doors and windows, steel joists and rods, bricks and mortar. Finally, out of such digested material, the body is built up. The town grows.

Now every stage in this digestive and body-building process has been guided by human beings. Lumbermen, miners, carpenters, ironworkers, architects, plumbers, and hosts of other experts, have directed the interior workings of the Earth-creature's body, shaping, choosing, planning, calculating, testing, organising. In other words — exercising their practical intelligence.

This practical intelligence is our strong point. We understand how to invent and run machines, to plan and erect buildings, to extract minerals from the earth, to manipulate matter in thousands of ways. Common-sense is at home in this sort of world. It belongs there, and it produces results there. But as soon as common-sense ceases to busy itself with the Earth-creature's body-building and body-maintenance, and tries to grasp the significance of what it is doing, then the difficulty arises.

We are just as efficient at helping the Earth-creature to live and grow, when we are unaware of its existence, as when we are aware.

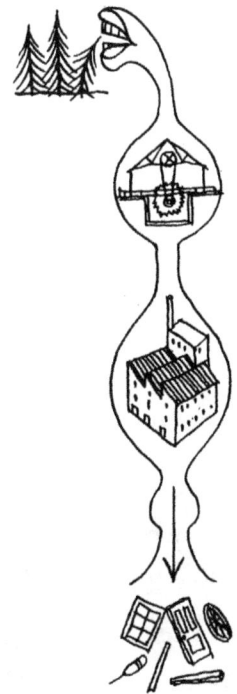

Our enlightenment does not improve its bodily condition, and perhaps that is the reason why enlightenment is so difficult to come by. Like the cells in our bodies, we are admirably fitted to function at our own particular level, and inexpert at appreciating what is going on at other levels. Your life means nothing to the cell inside you, yet its life is part and parcel of yours. Likewise the Earth-creature's life means little or nothing to you, yet you are part of it.

(The small arrows are meant to indicate the cells carrying on in their everyday work of keeping us going. The big arrows indicate ourselves doing the same thing, by means of practical intelligence, for the Earth-creature. And the dotted arrows indicate that faculty by which a man is able to escape from the prison of his everyday work to become aware of the Earth-creature of which he is part, and of the cell which is part of him.)

Has the Earth-creature a mind? And, if it has, is its mind anything like yours?

Now we know that it has a body, and we know that it is alive — if we get far enough away we can see it grow and do most of the things we see other living creatures do. But we cannot see its mind for the simple reason that minds are invisible.

There are two ways in which we can know about any particular mind: (1) by being that mind, and (2) by watching an object and seeing whether it acts as though it has a mind. Now your mind is obviously not the same thing as the Earth-creature's mind (if any), and it follows that, to get to know about the latter, we shall have to observe how the Earth-creature behaves as a whole. I say as a whole because the mind (again, if any) of the Earth-creature is not necessarily like the mind of one of its parts, any more than our minds are like our cells' minds, in so far as they can be said to have any.

Our question, then, amounts to this: does the Earth-creature as a whole act as though it has a mind?

To make sure, let us go back to our celestial observer's position, and see how the Earth-creature conducts itself when it is faced with a problem. We will give it an imaginary intelligence-test, based on the kind of test that is applied to apes. The intelligence of a chimpanzee

may be tested by putting a stick in his cage, and placing a banana outside the bars just beyond his reach; if he eventually picks up the stick and uses it to get the banana, he has shown intelligence; if he ignores the stick and goes on vainly reaching for the banana, he has failed to show intelligence.

In our test, we will place food, in the shape of a rich deposit of coal, well out of the Earth-creature's reach — on the further side of a river that is too deep and wide to send stalks over — and we will observe what happens.

The first thing we notice is an unusual vigour in the stalks near the river. Their sap becomes plentiful; they thicken; they form new stalk-clusters. It is as though the Earth-creature has seen what it wants, and is mustering strength to get it. Now a stupid creature would waste time and energy trying to send stalk after stalk over the river opposite the coal-deposit, and it would fail, because every time a stalk got a part of the way across it would be washed away. An intelligent ape turns his back on the banana he cannot reach, and goes to fetch a stick that will enable him to do so; and an intelligent Earth-creature would do much the same thing. Without making one false move, it would proceed up the near bank of the river, leaving its objective far behind, till it found a place where the river was narrow and could be crossed safely; then it would return down the further bank till it reached its goal. That precisely is what our Earth-creature does. Instead of rushing straight at its objective regardless of the consequences, it takes steps to attain its goal economically, with the minimum of effort. It adopts the indirect method. It exercises practical intelligence.

From our vantage point in the sky we can see many similar instances of intelligent behaviour on the Earth-creature's part. We can also see evidences of stupidity. Here are a few of them:

One of the staple diets of the Earth-creature is grass, which it eats by means of its sheep and cattle. Now grass-land soon becomes infertile if it is overworked, and an intelligent creature, having learned from bitter experience, would restrain its appetite. However hungry it felt, it would take the long view, and eat less today in order to leave something to eat tomorrow. The Earth-creature, in various parts of the world, has taken the short view, and is now reaping the conse-

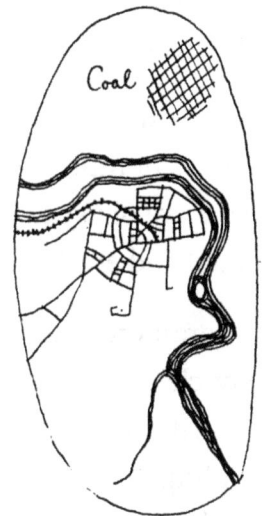

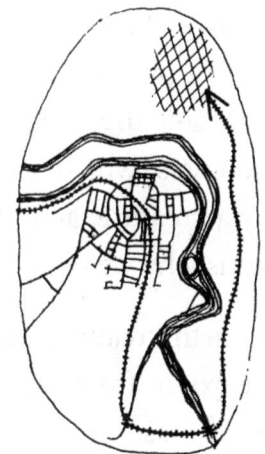

quences. In such matters it seems to be rather less intelligent than a man, who normally has the good sense to refrain from killing the goose that lays the golden egg, and even from killing the goose that lays the ordinary egg, preferring eggs for breakfast regularly to a single meal of roast goose.

Elsewhere the Earth-creature is thoughtlessly squandering its food supplies of timber and coal, impoverishing land, and killing off species that are of use to it. On the whole, its intelligence seems to be very limited and erratic.

Here common-sense disagrees: "This alleged Earth-creature is extremely clever. Observe the things it makes, from tramcars and television-sets, to an automatic telephone-exchange and the Empire State Building. If there is such a thing as this Earth-creature — which I do not admit — it is a genius."

The reply is this: A man's intelligence cannot be judged from the way he grows his eyes or his stomach — any dunce is as clever as a professor of physiology at that sort of thing. Neither can one judge the Earth-creature's intelligence from the way it grows tramcars and television-sets, which are organs of its body. Intelligence is seen in the way a creature, acting as a whole, deals with the outside world, and that is why we use bananas and coal deposits in our tests.

The Earth-creature, then, has a measure of intelligence. It learns to some extent from experience, and in a limited degree it exercises powers of reasoning. Obviously these mental powers are built up out of the organised human intelligence, and where the level of the Earth-creature's intelligence falls below ours, that is due to lack of proper mental organisation on our part. If the creature's practical intelligence is to be improved, it is we who will have to do it.

"And that," says common-sense, "is where I take you up again. Supposing this creature does exist, and is alive, and is intelligent up to a point, and supposing our lives make up its life, I hold it would still be disastrous for us to pay any attention to the thing. What is its life to us men? What happens to be good for it, may be bad for us. The safest course is to ignore it altogether and concentrate on human welfare, otherwise we — or, more likely, our rulers — will be in danger of

acting in its interests. Already individual man matters little enough. You would make him matter still less."

In other words, common-sense asks us to believe that it is safer to remain ignorant.

Surely, if there is any danger of our interests running counter to the 'interests' of the Earth-creature, that would be all the more reason why we should recognise the creature's existence. Playing the ostrich is not likely to help us, because, whether we approve or not, we are as deeply involved in the Earth-creature as our kidneys are involved in us.

No doubt our duty is towards men, and not towards the Earth-creature as such, though it is doubtful whether we are properly qualified to say exactly what the Earth-creature's welfare is. At any rate we can be sure of this: one of the most pressing duties of men at the moment is the eradication of the Earth-creature's three major internal diseases of war, extreme poverty in the midst of wealth, and aggressive nationalism. Here, if nowhere else, our interests are its 'interests'.

There is a sense in which human welfare does run counter to the Earth-creature's 'interests'. If these 'interests' are taken to include the creature's development into a more and more close-knit, more elaborately organised individual, in which men become specialists with ever-narrowing outlook, then our duty is to oppose these 'interests'. The main point to bear in mind is that, while awareness of the Earth-creature's existence may be a duty, the furtherance of its alleged or real welfare is not. It may very well turn out, however, that any apparent divergence of 'interests' is an illusion.

For when all is said, in spite of the wealth of our inside information the creature of whose body we are members remains mysterious. We happen to know a great deal about the way this body works, because our job is to help to work it; but what the creature amounts to as an individual — and particularly as a mind — we can never fully appreciate.

It is now clear that the view that we took of you in the last chapter, though correct as far as it went, was lop-sided. We saw your body as

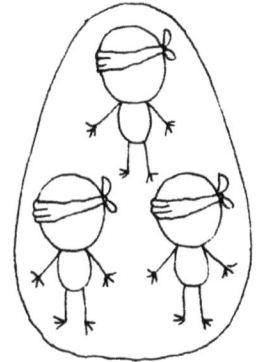

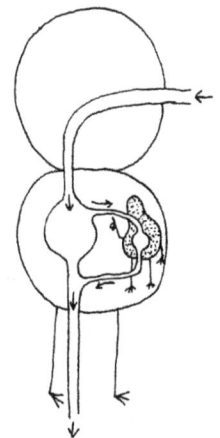

nothing less than the Earth-creature. No doubt the Earth-creature may be regarded as existing for your private benefit. But a supernaturally intelligent, self-centred cell in your body might, with equal justification, say to himself: "I must eat, otherwise I will die, and Jack Robinson exists to provide me with my food. He has a brain in order to earn money to buy this food, a stomach in which to digest it, and blood vessels to convey it to my doorstep. In fact, his brain as he thinks, his mouth as he feeds, his stomach as he digests, are mine, organs of my life, extensions of my body. Amputate any of them, and I die. I am Jack Robinson. And, being Jack Robinson, I am also his extensions. Ultimately, I am the whole of things!"

This self-centred cell would be telling the truth, and nothing but the truth. But not the whole truth. He should off-set this self-centredness by seeing himself as you see him — as a minute particle in a whole that is vastly greater than himself, a whole whose complete significance will always escape him.

So with yourself — except for one big difference. You can be conscious of the creature you are a minute part of, whereas your cells can never be conscious of you.

The cell is always subordinate to its Jack Robinson, but the immense range of Jack Robinson's consciousness enables him, in a very real sense, to rise superior to the being in whose body he lives. In that awareness lies our human triumph — in the awareness of our smallness no less than our vastness, in the awareness of our bondage to the thing that builds us and to the thing we build. No man is so captive as he who is unconscious of his chains, and awareness of bondage is the beginning of freedom.

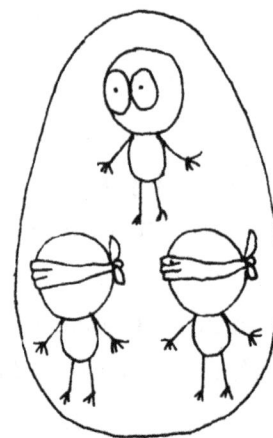

CHAPTER V

THE CAR SEED

"At least," says common-sense, "you must admit that I am (walking-city and Earth-creature notwithstanding) an individual. On that fact I take my stand. I am an individual human being, with all those qualities which distinguish man from animals, putting him in a class by himself. That is not boasting; it is observable fact."

Common-sense is always taking half-truths of this kind for the whole truth. In its every-day thinking, in its unspoken assumptions, it ignores the most elementary findings of science. It lacks awareness of what these findings mean, rather than knowledge of what they are. This lack is nowhere more evident than where our life, the phenomenon of our growth, and our status in the animal world are concerned.

Let us suppose you are thirty years old. Roughly thirty years nine months ago there lived a tiny animal — so tiny that it was invisible to the naked eye. Seen through a microscope, it would have looked something like an elongated tadpole, with a long thin tail which it swished energetically.

In bodily complexity and in mentality (if such a creature can be said to have any mind at all) it was inferior to most of the tiny animals that you can see swimming in stagnant water.

That 'tadpole' was you.

It happened that you came across another equally low form of life — a tail-less globular animal some hundreds of times bigger than yourself.

That creature was your other half.

Your two halves came together. The 'tadpole' drove its head into the tail-less creature and the two animals became one. You had started life as an individual.

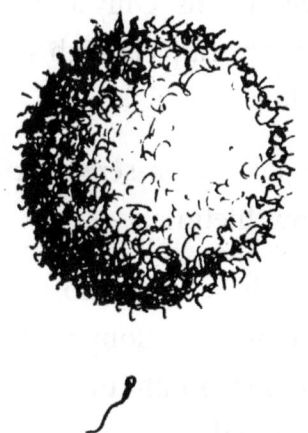

If plant-lice or water-fleas had met you at this stage of your career, they would have been perfectly justified in looking upon you as a very inferior animal, unworthy of their notice.

But you could afford to wait, for, unlike water-fleas, you had amazing potentialities. You grew — and how you grew! You grew into something like a very small jellyfish, then a distant relation of an earthworm, then a fishlike animal with the rudiments of gills. At a later stage you had something in common with reptiles. A social climber if ever there was one, you finally grew human. You were then born.

The history of the spermatozoon and the ovum (as the 'tadpole' and the globular creature are called) and of the development of the embryo in the womb, is common knowledge. But how far is it common awareness? How often do you realise that the fly on the window pane is immeasurably superior to you as you once were, in your own lifetime?

It is of no use to claim that, whatever happened before you were born, you started at birth, as a human being. You did not start at birth. You began your career as an individual nine months before you became human, and before that you lived in the bodies of your parents and forbears. Most of your years — and they are many — have been spent, not as one body but as many bodies, not as a human being but as a swarm of microscopic animals far lower in the life-scale than plant-lice. A really comprehensive record of you in your family photograph album would look like the illustrations of a book on disease germs. Only at the very end of your record would you rise to the comparatively high status of being jellyfish-like, worm-like, and fish-like.

But common-sense prefers to ignore all but the very last moments of your lifetime.

You have spent most of your career amongst the lowest forms of life; now you belong to the highest. The transformation, which took only nine months to complete, was surely a miracle. We call that miracle growth.

We give it a name, and think no more about it.

Familiarity breeds a deadly unawareness. The main reason why we are not awestruck when we think about growth is that there is so much of it. The growth of men and animals and plants is as common as dirt, and we are always falling into the error of thinking that what is as common as dirt cannot possibly be wonderful. It is only the rare which interests. We have head-line mentalities — anything unusual happens, like the birth of quintuplets, and we are agog with excitement. Quintuplets are, of course, surprising, but only such a tiny fraction more so than yourself that the difference in real amazement-value is negligible. Niagara Falls and the Empire State Building are really common-place beside a house-fly. And the Seven Wonders of the World only qualified as such because they were unusually big or dangerous-looking — as absurd a pair of incitements to true wonder as can be imagined.

We look at ourselves as an unimaginative archaeologist looks at buildings: when he walks into a Gothic cathedral, the beauty, the atmosphere, the fact of the cathedral, all escape his notice. What he does is to get excited over some minor piece of carving or a trivial inscription. Only the peculiar makes any impression on him. His very knowledge blinds him. So with many a gardener, who can recite the Latin name of every flower in the seed-catalogue, yet take every flower's growth and life for granted.

Suppose you lived on a planet inhabited only by permanently adult men who had never known anything to grow. And suppose, one day, you came across a seed and watched it grow a root and a stalk and green leaves, and finally — wonder of wonders! — you saw it burst into flower. What would you do? I think your impulse would be to fall down and worship it. It would seem to you to be a divine incarnation, a sublime and altogether miraculous being.

For the rest of your life you would be asking yourself how a little white pellet in a brown skin, when put into moist dirt, could possess the power to rush upwards and outwards, unfolding into such brilliant colours, such intricate patterns. You would not know whether to pity or despise people who, having counted the flower's petals and

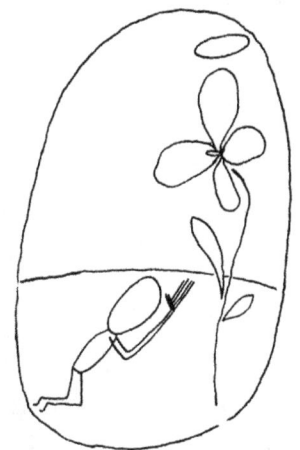

given it a Latin name, thought they had disposed of it. And if someone said he had an explanation of the new phenomenon, you would
ironically ask him to explain the Universe too.

All that would happen if there were only one flower. Are a billion
flowers so much less astonishing than one?

Time, no less than familiarity, makes for unawareness.

Growth is slow, as we count time. We do not see ourselves and
flowers grow; all we do is to make comparisons between what we see
today and what we remember having seen the other day. And we are
not specially impressed.

Now, while time seems to us to flow at a certain rate, it is not unlikely that for other minds time flows much more quickly, or much
more slowly. Imagine yourself for a moment to be a creature for
whom time flies, rather than walks or crawls. You have a flower-seed
in your hand. Having put the seed in a pot of dry earth, you add water
and await developments.

You do not have to wait long. Without warning, the earth opens
and a sort of jack-in-the-box springs up at you. For a split second you
glimpse delicate shapes flashing green and yellow and scarlet, a whiff
of perfume comes your way, then all vanishes. There lies the brown
earth as it was, with hardly a trace of the thing that came out of it.

That is what would happen if time were hurried up. But is something that takes five million seconds to happen so much less wonderful than the same thing when it happens in one second?

You and I are more remarkable than flowering plants. But because
we, like them, have grown slowly and in the company of millions of
our kind, we take ourselves for granted. Because the newspapers are
not interested in us as living things (but only as freaks or murderers
or politicians or film-stars), we accept ourselves at the news-editor's
valuation. And because scientists have written shelves of books about
the way you and I grew, and because their books are necessarily matter-of-fact treatises which refuse to become excited on the subject of
how extraordinary we are, we fail to see why we should either.

The scientist's job is to minimise his ignorance, not to estimate its extent. Nevertheless, he has, or should have, a very lively sense of the unknown, because the more he discovers about life the more unknowable it seems to be.

As an example, let us take the briefest of glances at what the text-books have to say about your growth. You grow, they say, much as a town grows — by increase in your population. At the age of minus nine months you were one tiny cell. This cell soon started to reduce its waist-line and bulge at its two ends. Its waist got smaller and smaller till it became nothing, and there were two cells. In the same way each of the two daughter cells split up, making a total of four cells, which split again and made eight. And so on, till you reached a grand to-tal of billions of cells. In your early stages, when you were only a few cells, they were of the same pattern, but as they multiplied they began to differ from each other in their bodies and to do different sorts of work. You are rather like a city founded by a farmer who had a large family of sons, some of whom remained farmers, while the rest took up the work of the farm's building and black-smithing and book-keeping. As the community grew bigger its needs increased; it had to have drainage inspectors and hardware merchants and civic officials, and every other sort of specialist. The grandsons and the great-grandsons of the founder rose to the occasion.

But there are many important distinctions between the way a city of men grows and the way you — a cell-city — grew. In particular, while the inhabitants of the one consciously take up their various trades and professions and more or less deliberately plan and build up their city, the inhabitants of the other built you unconsciously. When the members of your cell family started specialising — going in for posts and telegraphs, say, or police-work — they could not help themselves. Yet they went on specialising and multiplying to such an extent that they became your kidneys and your brain and your nerv-ous system and your eyes — till they became a machine that not only re-fuels itself, repairs itself, and steers itself, but one that sees, and remembers what it sees, and thinks about what it sees.

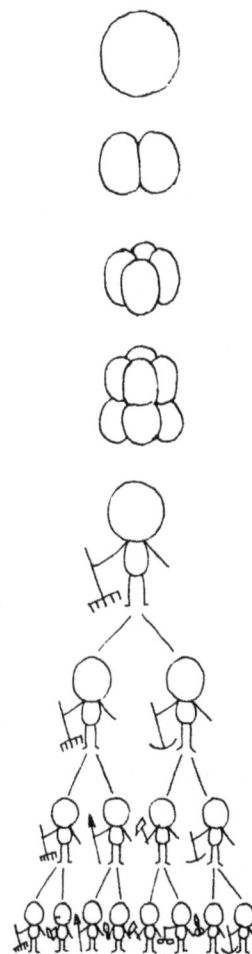

The parts of your body were much too stupid to know what they were doing when they grew themselves. They grew blindly and ignorantly, as a flower grows. Yet what sort of stupidity is it that can make a device like your eye without blue prints of it, and can make the brain that is conscious of the self and the world, without taking lessons in half-a-dozen-ologies? What sort of ignorance is it that knows how to grow, almost out of nothing, a machine whose intricacies are inexhaustible?

You see what happens when we try to 'explain' growth — we only multiply the need for further explanations. Science does not know how or why a cell has the art of dividing into two cells. It does not know how or why the two cells are clever enough to multiply further, and, multiplying, to grow into nerve cells and brain cells. It does not know how or why nerves and brains can be such incredible geniuses at their jobs.

A modern car is a remarkable device, yet to achieve the same degree of remarkableness as yourself it would need some such history as this:-

Wishing to possess a car, you go, not to a manufacturer, but to a seedsman, and you buy from him a seed that is no bigger than a speck of dust. You place it on a bed of earth manured with steel filings, and wait.

The seed grows. At first it appears to be no more than an expanding metallic pellet, but as it gets bigger it begins to resemble a cart, then a coach, then one of the primitive cars of the early twentieth century — these transformations taking place gradually, so that one stage merges with the next. Day by day the lines of the car become more and more modern, till finally you have before you the latest model, oiled, greased, fuelled, and running with perfect smoothness.

You get in and go for a ride. And you find that the car is not only able to steer itself and change gears at exactly the right moment, but to mend its own punctures, and recharge its own batteries, and refine its own petrol from crude oil, and even read its own maps. It can discuss with you the best route to take, and the state of weather. It can build its own garage and bring up a family. It can talk to you about cars, and the mystery of their growth from tiny metal seeds, and their place in the scheme of things.

You would be surprised. And, even if you were a brilliant motor-mechanic, you would not dream that you knew how your car came to be a car, or what it really was.

All that this imaginary machine achieved, you and I have achieved in actuality. All that it was, we are. How, then, can we claim to know anything (beyond a few almost irrelevant and entirely superficial details) about ourselves? How can we, in every mood and in all things, continue to take ourselves for granted?

CHAPTER VI

THE THRICE-BORN BODY

Let us continue to assume that you are thirty years old. Common-sense admits, I think, that to this thirty years must be added the nine months you spent in your mother's womb, before we arrive at the date of your real birthday.

"Agreed," says common-sense. "Thirty years nine months behind me, and another thirty or forty years ahead of me if I am lucky — that is the span of my life. Leaving aside what religion has to say about my soul's future (the wish for immortality is, I suspect, the father of the doctrine), seventy years or so sees the start and the finish of me. Life is like that, and the statement in the last chapter about my having led some kind of previous existence in my parents' bodies carries no conviction."

But as soon as you think about the way you began life thirty years nine months ago, it is clear that you did not begin life at all. You merely appeared in a new form.

Let us go over the details once again.

You began your present phase as a single tiny fertilised cell, which presently grew fat, thinned down in the middle, and became two cells. The two cells repeated the process and became four. And the doubling and redoubling went on till you became millions of millions of cells.

Every cell in your body, then, is a fragment of your original cell.

But this original cell was a union of two cells, one (the 'tadpole') from your father and the other (the tail-less creature) from your mother.

And these two cells, in turn, were fragments of the original cells of your father and of your mother.

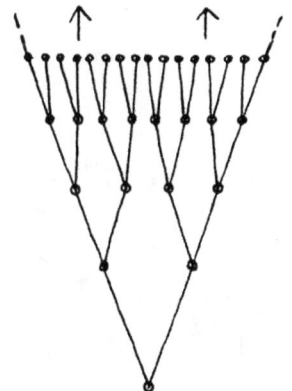

And the original cells of your father and mother were fragments of the original cells of your four grandparents, which were fragments of the original cells of your eight great-grandparents, and so on.

Five hundred years ago your ancestors probably numbered hundreds of thousands (even after we have allowed for marriages between cousins), and your body is actually an overgrown bit of each of their bodies — the bit that survived when the rest died, and now survives in you.

Of course the material of your present body is not the material which your ancestors handed on, any more than it is the material of the body you were born with, because a constant stream of food passes through each cell, gradually replacing it.

This fact of replacement, however, does not alter your conviction that your body of the moment is your body of twenty years ago. If that conviction is a reasonable one, it is equally reasonable to say that your body was present and alive five hundred years back in the bodies of hundreds of thousands of men, women, and children — princes and paupers, courtiers and peasants, foreigners and your own countrymen. History has an added interest when you realise the fact that it is, in a very real sense, your history.

This diagram will help to show how your body spreads out into the past, through the bodies of your ancestors:

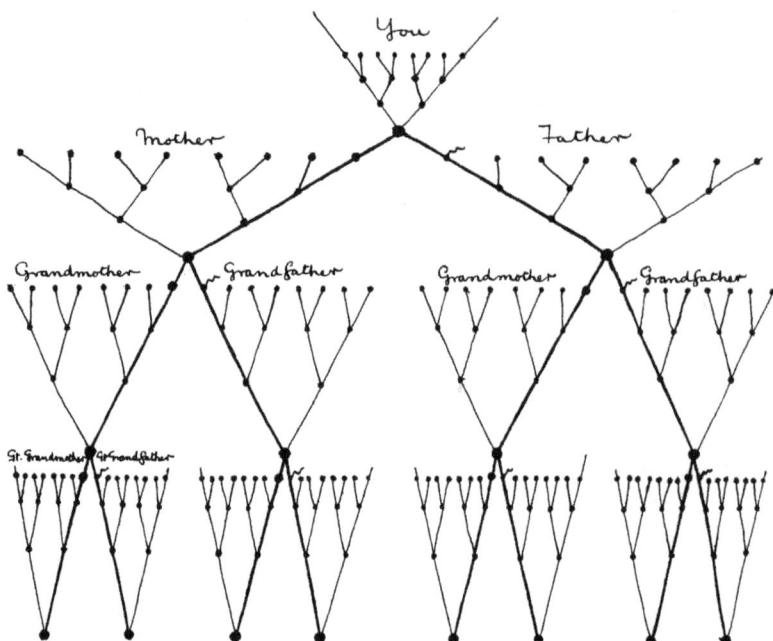

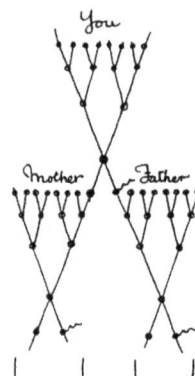

The thick lines indicate the life-line (so to speak) which connects your present compact body with your past distributed body. The thin lines indicate those portions of your ancestors' bodies which split off from you, and either died, or survived in children which were not forbears of yours. Allowance must of course be made for the fact that, whereas I have only room enough to show fifteen or so cells per body, there are millions of millions, and whereas I have shown your family tree (it is an inverted family tree) stopping with your great-grandparents, it really goes back hundreds, thousands, millions of generations…

Back to what?

Your forbears some hundreds of thousands of years ago were hairy men with low foreheads, and their forbears were animals like monkeys that lived in the trees, and their forbears were reptiles, and their forbears were fish, and their forbears were a very primitive kind of animal that lived in water, and their forbears were tiny single cells.

Inside the bodies of all these forbears of yours, and inside the bodies of all the intermediate forms of life that I have left out, you lived.

Consider what experience you have had in your life-time — in all the millions of years of it. Think what myriads of bodies you have inhabited. Think how travelled you are. Think how much of the soil you tread on, and of the air you breathe, and of the water you drink, must have passed through your distributed body before this, and have become for a time part of your life. What material for an autobiography is here!

But there was a time when there was no life on Earth. Somehow, perhaps two or three thousand million years ago, life was born out of dead matter.

What the earliest living things were like we can only guess. Probably they were very small and simple compared with even the simplest of the creatures that we know, yet they were able to grow by taking nourishment, and to beget creatures like themselves by splitting their bodies when they became inconveniently big.

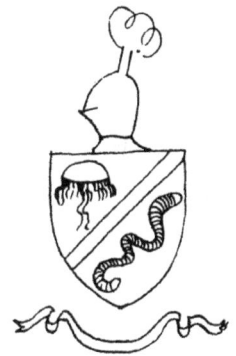

Such creatures were your greatest-grandparents. When they were born out of dead matter, you were born, for your body was enshrined in theirs. You are bits of their bodies that have gone on splitting and spreading themselves for millions of generations.

It would require an almost infinitely big sheet of paper to show in just how many bodies and in just how many kinds of animals you were distributed. But there came a time when you started to contract, eventually restricting yourself to sixteen great-great-grandparents, to eight great-grandparents, to four grandparents, to your father and mother, until, on your second birthday, you were concentrated in a single cell. From that crisis in your life onwards you began spreading again till, on your third or human birthday, you numbered millions of millions of little bodies which, as a novelty, were stuck together instead of being scattered over the wide world.

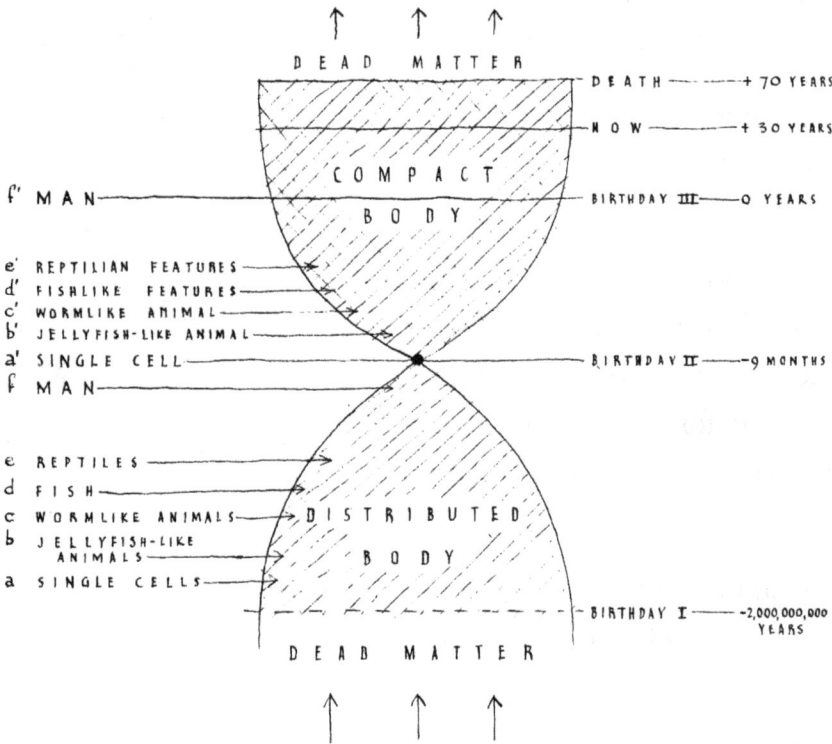

In Chapter V we saw how you took up your residence as a single cell in your mother's womb, and in that restricted space grew till you became something like a jellyfish, a worm, a fish, a reptile, and eventually a human being. Our diagram indicates this phase of your career which you spent in one body and in one place; it indicates also the previous phase which you spent in many bodies and in many places.

Observe how the later phase of your career repeats the earlier: your life from your first birthday to your second is a slow-motion version of your life from your second to your third or human birthday. It is as if, when you were growing in the womb, you remembered your previous lives in the scattered bodies of countless creatures, and modelled the development of your compact body on the pattern of their scattered bodies. You started your one-body life as a single cell because you had once been a host of single cells. You became a 'jellyfish' in the womb because you had once lived in animals resembling jellyfish. As a 'worm' in the womb you reflected your worms' constitution outside. You developed imitation gills as an embryo in remembrance of the real gills of the fish that you once inhabited.

You have evolved, in piecemeal form, from cell to man, and you have repeated the process in your compact body. The first evolution took you, say, 2,000,000,000 years; the second you accomplished in nine months. Your biography includes, not only that stupendous unfolding known as evolution, but evolution twice over.

What happened on that first birthday of yours, some thousands of millions of years ago? Did certain pieces of dead matter, or possibly one piece, suddenly become infused with life?

It seems unlikely. More probably life had no definite beginnings, but rose by such easy stages from the dead that for us to talk of the first living creatures is meaningless. If this was so, and bits of dead matter gradually became more and more complicated and more and more like living bodies till they really were alive, then your greatest grandparents were at least half dead. And you, enshrined in their bodies, were no more than half alive.

But your past does not stop in some no-man's-land between life and death. These greatest-grandparents of yours evolved out of less complicated material that was certainly dead, and through them you spread back beyond life to the world of ordinary molecules and

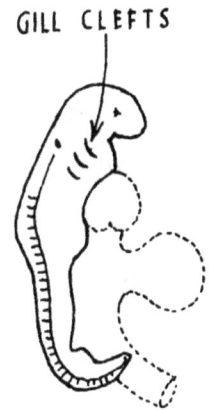

atoms. There is a sense in which you indwelt the rocks and water of the Earth long before life began. You were present when this planet was a cloud of hot gas torn out of the Sun by the attraction of a passing star. When the Earth was part of the Sun you were there. Ultimately you are co-existent with the stuff of the Universe.

So much for your past. What of your future?

If you have children, a part of your body will live on in them. In that way you may go on living and spreading yourself for thousands and millions of years to come.

But if you have no children — what then? Do you vanish entirely?

No. You will go on and on as long as the universe functions. Only you will get more and more scattered, and therefore more and more diluted, till you become so unlike the thing you know as yourself that only God Himself will be capable of recognising you.

Everything you do changes the future of the world. That favourite story of the physics-teacher about the Earth jumping up to meet the pin you drop to the floor, is sober truth. Every time you drop a pin, or walk about, or breathe, or do anything at all with your body, you disturb the world in a thousand ways, and in places you will never see. You do not have to be a Wren or a Ferdinand de Lesseps to change the face of things. You cannot help affecting the history of the Universe. The Universe will never recover from you.

In this sense all men have physical immortality; their least-considered deeds go on influencing events long after the death of their flesh-and-blood bodies.

Then there is that other sort of immortality which we associate with the names of famous artists and thinkers. There is a sense in which their minds are still at work enriching your mind and mine, as well as influencing our behaviour. In a smaller way each of us leaves behind some contribution to the sum total of human thought and feeling, and that contribution will go on producing effects while men continue to live.

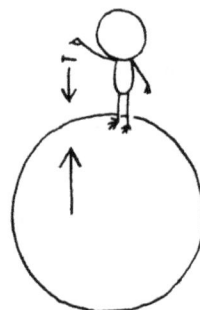

Finally, it is conceivable that the flow of time is in the last resort an illusion, and no more than the means by which our limited minds can know a timeless world. This world may be like a cinema film: when the reel is taken from its container and put through the projector, we experience the beginning, the development, and the climax of the story. But the film neither began with its screening nor ended with it; the complete reel, comprising every incident in the story, was present in the cinema all the time. So may your life-story, which seems to consist of a beginning, a development, and a climax, be in reality timeless, or co-existent with the universe.

At this stage we can well imagine that common-sense has something to say:

"This so-called immortality is far too nebulous to have any attraction for the matter-of-fact man. In a hundred years' time there will, no doubt, still be traces of the way I laid out my garden; there will be one more tombstone in the cemetery than there would have been had I never lived; I may even have great-great-grandsons (they will probably never have heard of me) to my name.

In short, the material of the world will doubtless be arranged a little differently because of my having lived. But I — my body — will not be present in any shape or form. Nor, for that matter, will my mind.

"It is just the same with my past, as you call it. Of what use is a body distributed among shoals of fish and cart-loads of monkeys, or enshrined in half the population of the country? Call that sort of thing immortality if you must — it is too vague to mean anything to me, and certainly it is cold comfort to the dying.

"Finally, what is the value of a doubtful immortality in a possibly timeless universe, while my mind is anything but timeless?"

There is a great deal in the common-sense view. (Incidentally, there always is something; but there is never enough). This bodily immortality we have been considering is a nebulous, shadowy thing. But then, if you are searching for well-defined facts, for clear-cut realities, where will you find them?

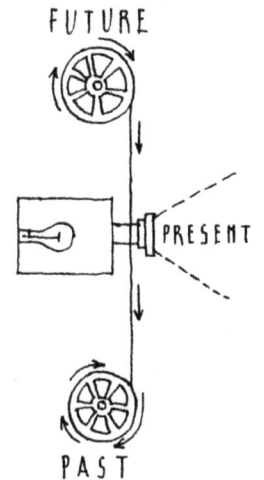

In your present body?

Will you find them in this walking city, with its myriads of little unconscious citizens, with its extensions that embrace the globe, with its membership of a vast Creature? Will you find them in the little quick-change artist that played his extraordinary parts in the womb? Or in the hundred and fifty pounds of your present body, which is not made of the material you were born with, which has no definite boundaries, whose growth, and functioning, and very life, are past all finding out?

You will not. The millions of years of your past are nebulous, and the millions of years of your future are nebulous. But so is your present.

CHAPTER VII

THE SCATTERED BODY

In Chapter III we saw how, by growing a colossal outer body capable of painless and piecemeal amputation, you extend yourself in space till you cover the Earth. That picture of you, we decided, was a true likeness, but only one of many likenesses. The camera was close to you, and of course you dominated the picture. To correct any false impressions we took a distant view of you, and then you appeared as a sort of tiny cell in the Earth-creature.

In the previous chapter we have seen you stretching out in time instead of space, till your age has to be reckoned in millions of years. This picture too is a likeness, but it is also a 'close-up'. We must now take a more distant view and see your past as merging with the past of countless living things.

Your greater body of the present is not yours alone, neither is your greater body of the past yours alone: you share it with myriads of creatures.

Accordingly we must draw your family tree thus:-

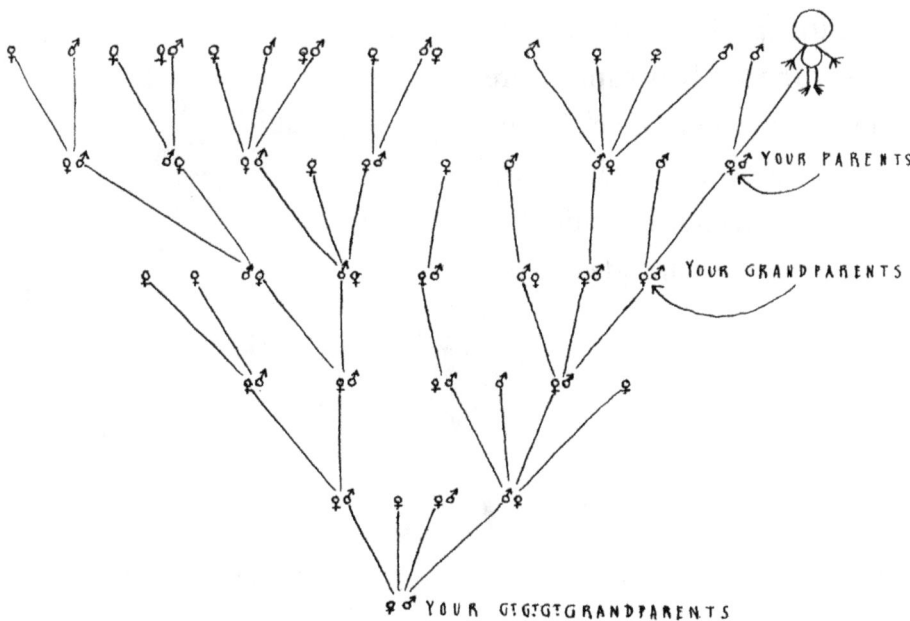

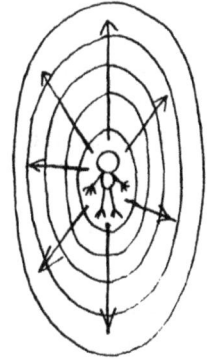

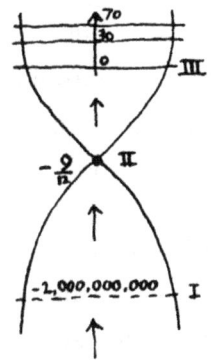

Imagine this drawing multiplied millions of times so that it goes back to your remote forbears, back to your sub-human, ape-like, reptilian ancestors, back to your greatest grandparents.

Notice how, in the previous chapter, you crown the past; your present body is the common stem towards which all the branches and twigs converge. And notice how, in this chapter, you are as it were a tiny leaf, of no particular consequence, on the tree of life.

You are a microscopic piece of Life. And by Life I do not mean an abstraction, or some mystical entity. I refer to a single Creature, having one Body of which you are part.

Common-sense will certainly object here. "Life, with or without the capital initial, is certainly not one body. It is millions and billions of bodies having no connection with one another."

Admittedly Life's body is vastly different from your body and mine. In particular, it has failed to grow up as one compact piece and instead has grown up as an incalculable number of separate pieces, of which you are one.

But this scattered Body in which you belong is like ordinary compact bodies in a number of important ways. For one thing it grew up from single cells much as you did. And as it grew its parts became more and more unlike one another (in other words, more and more kinds of animals and plants appeared on the scene) in much the same way as your cells developed into little specialists, doing duty as muscle cells, brain cells, and all the rest. The Body became more and more elaborate, much as you became more and more elaborate as you grew in the womb. The way the Body grew is usually shown something like this, though needless to say the diagram, besides being extremely inaccurate, can give no more than a faint idea of the complexity of the process.

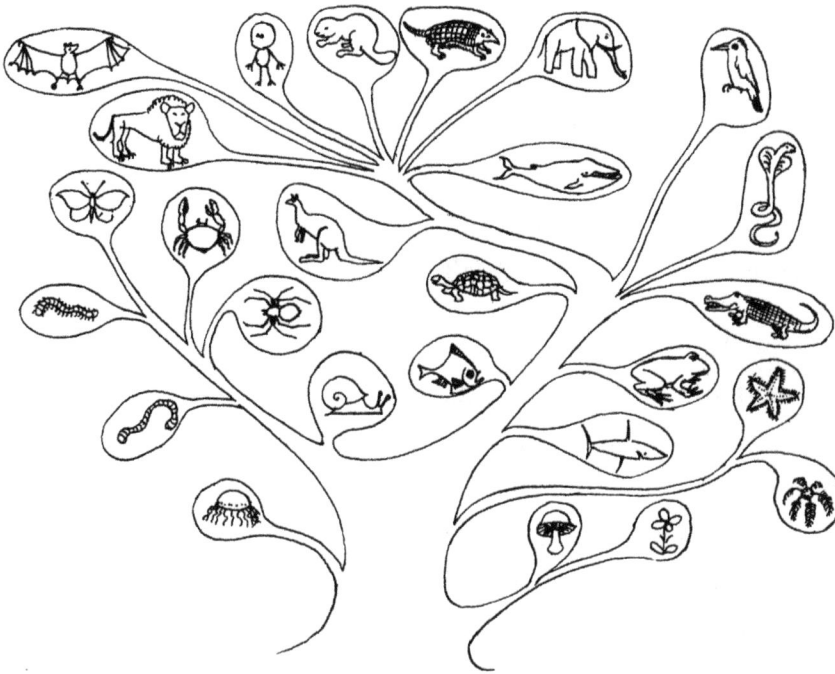

"You say," says common-sense, "that we living creatures are parts of a Body which has grown up from our common cell-ancestors, in much the same way as my cells are parts of my present body, which has also grown up from cell-ancestors. I cannot agree, and this is my reason: on the one hand, the parts of my body are all dependent on one another; they are so bound up together in one bundle of life that none of them has any real life or meaning apart from the bundle. On the other hand, animals and plants and men, which according to you form the organs of one Body, live their own lives independently of each other. We may all have come from common greatest-grandparent cells, but we have gone our own ways, and remained entirely separate individuals."

Again common-sense is partly right. No doubt this Body is a loose-jointed affair. No doubt great distances divide its parts. No doubt the creatures which are its organs and cells (so to speak) have far more independence than your organs and cells have, so that only by exercising imagination can we think of the Body as a whole.

All the same, living creatures are not independent of each other. They too are bound up in one bundle of life, and, though the bundle is loosely tied, the cords that bind it are strong.

Let us take one or two instances, out of the thousands that could be taken, of the mutual dependence of the Body's parts.

All living things need for their growth and sustenance certain chemical constituents of the soil. Plants can feed on these substances directly and without help, whereas animals cannot do so. It would be useless for us to send roots down into the soil, or to chew mouthfuls of it, because we lack the apparatus for turning the soil's mineral salts into body-building material.

The vegetable kingdom has a corner in this essential apparatus, which it generously employs in turning out, not only its own requirements, but the food supply of the entire animal kingdom into the bargain. We live because we are kept supplied with prepared food (in the shape of roots, stems, leaves, flowers and fruit) by chemical laboratories that build, equip, and run themselves, and whose trade formulae we have yet to discover.

In other words, the animals in Life's Body are as dependent upon the plants in the Body as your brain is dependent upon your stomach. But the obligations are not all on one side. In many ways plants have come to rely upon animals. Flowering plants give a striking instance of this dependence.

If there were no bees or other insects there would be no flowers. Plants have developed the art of growing that vast mass of advertising material which we call flowers, with their brilliant colours and fantastic shapes, with their scents and their nectar pockets, solely to attract insects.

The plant needs the bee to assist in its sex-life, and pays, for services rendered, in the shape of nectar and pollen, without which the bee cannot live. The bee and the plant can no more dispense with each other than your head can dispense with your trunk. The bee's life and structure and the flower's life and structure, when seen apart, lack meaning. Their life patterns have become one.

In varying measure, what is true of bees and flowers is true throughout Nature. Species mould each other's lives and forms, within a gigantic life-pattern. They are mutually dependent in behaviour and structure. Seen thus, Life has the requisites of unity. It is one Body.

But within this Body there is struggle as well as mutual aid. How can Nature, red in tooth and claw, always at war with herself, yet be one Body?

Oddly enough, this internal strife has tended towards unity. On the whole, the struggle has made for an ever-increasing number of types whose lives are more and more elaborately adjusted to one another. The law of the survival of the fittest (that is, of the most perfectly adjusted) has served, not to disintegrate Life's Body, but to regulate its vital processes and to further its growth. Just as our own bodies are maintained only by constant internal struggle, in which the opposing forces are finely balanced, so is Life's Body maintained.

This, then, is the situation: though the parts of the Body have remained apart, thus preserving a measure of independence that is more apparent than real, invisible bonds still make the parts one. The Body, though scattered, is still one Body, and you are a tiny portion of it.

How much do you, as an individual, matter in this Body?

To answer this question a digression is necessary.

The Body is hundreds of millions of years of age, and still growing. Now it is difficult for us to form a clear idea of how such a long-lived body grows, unless we imagine time flowing very swiftly. Let us, therefore, think of the Body as growing a million times faster than it appears to us to grow. What do we find?

Instead of individuals like you and me and your dog and an oak tree, we find types of animals and plants — the dog-type and the oak-tree-type, for instance. Time flows far too quickly for us to glimpse individuals as they rush by.

The types form a vast family of very mixed quality. Some members of it are so minute that they cannot be seen even under a high-powered microscope, and are correspondingly stupid. Other members are as big as houses, but not brilliant in proportion. Amongst both the small and the bigger children there are those who seem as though they will never grow up, and those who, instead of growing up, get smaller and smaller. There are some children that turn out badly, get fatter and lazier every day, batten on their relations, and often pro-

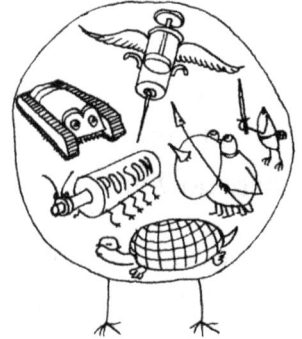

duce children that are more indolent than themselves. And there are young hopefuls in this family, who grow wonderfully and out of all recognition. They develop active bodies, and keen eyesight, and large brains, and, when they divide up, their children are sometimes more brilliant still.

This family is Life's Body, seen as consisting of types (or species, genera, and families) of animals and plants, instead of individuals. But where do you, an individual, figure in such a Body?

You scarcely figure at all. It is Man the species (that infant prodigy of the family) that counts, rather than man the individual. It is Man's growth, from a babyhood spent as a hairy creature with a broad nose and no tools, to the strange adolescence he is now passing through, and from the miseries of youth to (let us hope) a civilised adult life — it is his growing-up that matters, not your little growing-up and mine. It is the enrichment of Man's mind which all art and science serve; the fact that you and I can enjoy some of that mind's wealth is of little importance.

You are a 'cell' which is here today and gone tomorrow, a cell tiny almost to the point of invisibility, within a growing organ called Man. And this organ is a limb of Life. And Life has one Body. It is one Creature.

What happens to that minute bit of the Creature which goes by the name of Jack Robinson, hardly matters. You are too ineffective and transient to count. Whether you live or die, or understand why you are living or dying, or know the Creature in which you have life, the Creature will go on almost the same as if you had never been.

But your insignificance does not mean you are left out in the cold by Life. You are only a minute part of its Body, but all of you is part. Your life is as much a part of its life as a leaf's life is part of its branch's life and its tree's life. You may ignore the stalk that connects you with your Branch, and the Tree may be out of sight and so out of mind; nevertheless leaf, Branch, Trunk and Root are members of one Body, and share one Life.

This is sober fact, and a mystery only in the sense that everything is mysterious underneath.

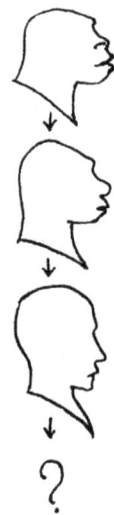

CHAPTER VIII

THE EMPTY BODY

How much remains of common-sense's estimate of you?

What we have seen of your membership of vaster bodies, of your lack of boundaries, of the extent of your past, and of the problems of your present, has stripped you of nearly every familiar trait. But at least there is left a core, a residue at the centre. You, as a body of flesh and bone, have become transformed under our scrutiny, but you have not melted away. Something solid and substantial, weighing a hundred and fifty pounds, tangible and evident, remains.

And yet, in reality, you are practically nothing but empty space.

You consist of an enormous number of tiny living creatures called cells. And each cell consists of an enormous number of tiny dead particles called molecules. And each molecule consists of atoms. And atoms, we are told, consist of electrons and protons. And electrons and protons are something electrical. And electricity is — well, electricity just is.

Scientists do not as a rule attempt to picture what an atom is like; instead, they try to describe its behaviour in mathematical terms. To us who find their marks on paper meaningless, and insist on something we can visualise, scientists offer, rather grudgingly and with reservations, a picture of the atom that is like this:

The atom is almost empty — a void. At the centre of the void lies a speck of electricity, and at the circumference lie anything from one to ninety-two specks of electricity of a different kind. These outer specks revolve about the central one in circles and ellipses at an enormous speed, like planets revolving round a sun.

To convey an idea of how empty the atom is: 25,000 of the outer specks put end to end would be required to reach from the outside of the atom's space to its centre; and the speck at the centre is of the same order of size as the outside ones. If an atom were enlarged till it was as high as the Empire State Building, or two and a half times as

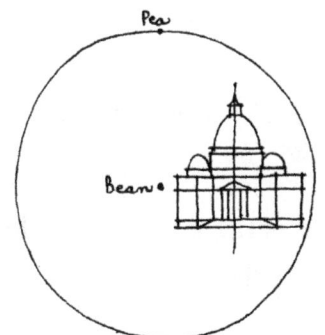

high as the dome of St. Peter's at Rome, its electron specks would be the size of peas, and its central speck would be rather larger — call it a bean. The rest would be empty space. If all the electrical specks in your body were gathered together into a lump, the lump would be so small as to be invisible to the naked eye. Even so, it would not be what we ordinarily mean by solid.

You are, in fact, a great emptiness sparsely dotted with 'suns', round which 'planets' are ceaselessly whirling. To a sufficiently tiny man of science you would resemble a problem in astronomy rather than one in biology. It is hardly an exaggeration to say that you have more in common with the Milky Way than with the common-sense's picture of you as a solid mass of flesh and bone.

Not only your body, but the whole of the world's 'substance' is made this way — out of electrical specks and nothingness. Earth, men, trees, stars, and tramcars boil down to a sort of speckled void, and even the specks are so queerly behaved and indefinite that scientists have given up trying to picture what they are like, and content themselves with writing equations on paper. The equations give information, of a kind, about atoms and electrons and radiation, much as temperature charts give information, again of a kind, about hospital patients: the symbols have their uses, but they are no more than symbols.

A silent and colourless world, empty save for specks of electricity that tear meaninglessly around in it, pointless, purposeless, soul-less — what sort of world is this? Where in such a drab nightmare of a Universe is there a place for you and for the things you value? How do flowers and sunsets and your friends, and your thoughts as you read this page, and all the rest that you know as real, come into such a picture?

They arrive by a kind of miracle, or rather by an unending series of miracles. The miracles cannot be explained; they can only be described. One description, much condensed, is as follows:

The electrical specks are, so to speak, the raw material, and the world is the finished article. What happens between the one and the other is the result of sociability.

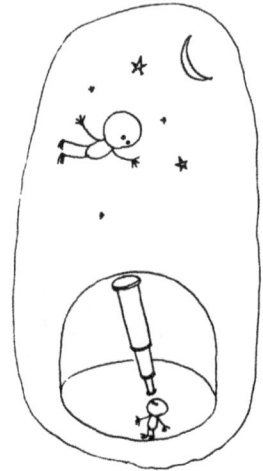

For the electrical specks, indeterminate though they appear to be, by no means ignore one another. Being socially inclined, they come together in exclusive societies having a membership of anything between two and several scores, and each society we call an atom. Now the odd thing is not so much that this society, with its intricate code of rules or social pattern, should form itself, but that it should behave so differently from its members when they are loose. It is the habit of individual electrons to whirl round a nucleus, or more rarely, to shoot off into space. The atom, on the other hand, has quite different habits from its members, and is a totally different sort of individual. For instance, it acts as though it were a solid particle, and, as a rule, it shows a marked affinity for certain other atoms.

Atoms, in their turn, are 'sociable'. They also form societies, called molecules, whose behaviour is unique. For example, when two hydrogen atoms get intimately involved with one oxygen atom, the three atoms become a molecule of water. Now water is very different from hydrogen (which is the gas that is put in balloons), from oxygen (which forms part of the air about us), and from a mere mixture of the two. Somehow water has emerged out of not-water, and nobody knows quite how it happened.

Though the bulk of your body is made up of only a few kinds of atoms, it contains many kinds of atom-societies, or molecules. The water molecules in your cells, the calcium phosphate molecules in your bones, the molecules of acid which help you to digest your food, are three examples, and each kind of molecule has new qualities that cannot be found in its atom members.

You are, then, so many ounces of water, acid, calcium phosphate, and other chemical substances. Already, thanks to this universal habit of sociability, we have arrived in a world which is familiar, though it is still a long way removed from the living.

How dead molecules can form a living cell is one of the greatest of all problems, and furnishes a striking instance of how unpredictable are the results of sociability. A cell is a gigantic molecule society, consisting of countless millions of members, each of which is dead.

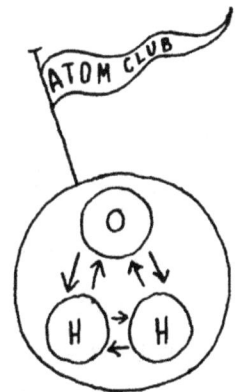

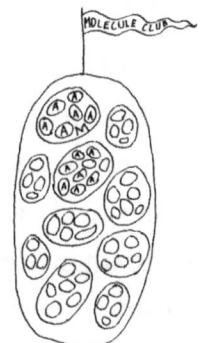

These members are of different sizes and composition, and their behaviour towards one another obeys social rules which are extremely elaborate; but however numerous these members, and however complicated their mutual relations, the fact that they are dead as individuals, yet alive as a corporate body, remains a mystery.

We have already, in Chapter II, noticed the miracle of how you, with your human feelings, your self-consciousness, your intelligence, arrive out of the sociableness of your stupid, un-selfconscious cells.

And finally we saw in Chapter IV how the Earth-creature, which is neither a Man, nor a Plant, nor an Animal, nor a Machine, is the result of the sociableness of you and me and the rest of men, along with our extensions.

Of course, the Earth-creature is not the final whole. It can be looked on as a member of the Earth; the Earth as member of our Solar System, our Solar System as part of the Universe.

We now have, in barest outline, a picture of the world you belong to. It starts with empty space sparsely dotted with specks called electrons and protons, and it ends with empty space sparsely dotted with specks called stars. Somewhere in between, you and I put in an appearance, and the familiar world emerges. We know very little about how it emerges, except that the sociability of things — of atoms for atoms, of molecules for molecules, of cells for cells, of men for men, and so on — works miracles of world-building. Somehow this 'sociability' has achieved in the process such qualities as life, mind, and self-consciousness. And, somehow, it has achieved you.

I have a notion of what you are like, and ordinarily I take that notion to be true; in actual fact it is so narrow a view of the truth about you as to amount to an illusion.

To take only one example, what you appear to me to be depends upon my size. If, like Alice in Wonderland, I could nibble at a mushroom which would enable me to grow or diminish at will, I would see you under many aspects. Imagine, for instance, that I am growing from less-than-electron size to more-than-star size, and that, throughout my growth, I am equipped with the same kind of eyes and brain as at present. What do I see?

To begin with, I see you as a great emptiness gradually solidifying, as I grow, into a world of dead particles. Matter has arrived, but as yet there is no life. Then I see the particles get smaller and melt away into vast changing shapes, which, ever diminishing, reveal themselves at last as parts of the bodies of stupid gigantic creatures — shoals of them. These creatures, living cheek by jowl, eat, reproduce themselves, and die, and each of them is obsessed with his private problem of keeping himself alive. As soon as this unpleasing menagerie begins to shrink sufficiently, I observe that the animals are not promiscuously jumbled, but live in big and small colonies. Colonies of one sort of creature, I find, are this shape, of another sort, that shape. As the creatures go on diminishing and eventually become invisible, I can see only the patterns that their massed bodies make — branching threads, tubes, pouches, jungle-like growths, and streams. I wonder whether I am looking at a very peculiar countryside. After a time it dawns upon my amazed consciousness that the landscape has the form of a man, alive and like myself. It is the you I know.

But the man soon becomes pigmy, a homunculus, a speck, and then disappears. Where he has been standing I see another sort of landscape, and in the centre of this new landscape a great Creeper which glows at night, breathes out smoke, branches outwards in all directions, and is gifted with intelligence. The man that I was looking at is evidently a mere particle within this Creeper.

Vast though it is, the Creeper fades from sight as the Earth dwindles like a pricked balloon. In the end, the Earth itself is invisible, and I see only the Sun, as a bright grain of dust in a dust-cloud that is whirling through space.

I am now grown up. When I started growing, the world was empty save for a fine 'dust' that was in it. Now I am adult the world is much the same again. But what a vision I had as I grew.

That vision is you.

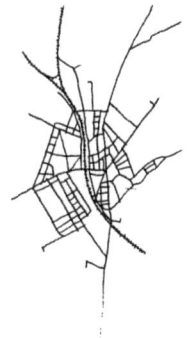

CHAPTER IX

THE ONE-MAN SHOW

At the beginning of this book we found that, because all you can be aware of are the ideas in your mind, you cannot know what the 'outside' world is like. Common-sense disagreed, and insisted that you do know what this 'outside' world is like, and that it is a material affair. Accordingly, from Chapter II onwards, we assumed that common-sense was right in this respect if in no other, and we took the world at its face value, as a world of matter.

But matter, as we discovered in the previous chapter, ultimately consists of electrical specks and space, and does not remotely resemble common-sense's notion of it. Its colour, and shape, and solidity have disappeared, and we are left with little else but mathematical formulae. For common-sense there is now only a choice between evils: between a world made of ideas, and a world made of electrical specks whirling in a great emptiness.

Even the electrical specks are queerly indefinite. Sometimes they behave like waves, at other times like particles. It seems that scientists are free to look upon them as either, according to which alternative happens to fit a particular case of behaviour. It is as though the observer's view-point and the nature of the electron are inseparable. Some scientists even go so far as to suggest that electrons are in some sense a creation of mind. This opinion seems less rash when we remember that we can be quite sure of the existence of mind (since we are minds), whereas matter is really an assumption.

If there is any truth in the foregoing, then our wheel has come full circle. Whether we choose to regard your world as a system of ideas or a system of matter, the result is the same: your world is ultimately built of mind-stuff.

Similarly with yourself: you may prefer to look upon your body as a material thing (that is, as an electron swarm), or as a set of ideas — in either case it seems that your body is, in the last resort, a mental and not a material affair.

We return, then, to the view that you are a mind, and that, for you, your body is a complicated system of ideas in that mind.

We have already decided that your mind does not belong in space. It is neither big nor small, and it has neither shape nor colour. It is not situated inside your head nor outside your head. It is nowhere. (If you have any doubt about this, consider how much room the fear of spiders takes up in your mind, or how many inches long your ideas about food are, or whether your love of country lies north or south of the dream you had last night). You are your mind; it follows that you are this shapeless, colourless, weightless thing that is nowhere.

Common-sense might conclude that we have now argued you out of existence altogether. Actually, we have done nothing of the sort. It does not follow that because you are nowhere you do not exist. You do not belong in space, but you do belong in a perfectly real world — in a world which has no room in it, and needs no room, because its 'contents' are not extended in space.

And of what do you, as a spaceless mind, consist? You consist of equally spaceless pictures. These pictures — of stars, and tramcars, and your body, and of spiders, and food, and the contents of dreams — are the raw material of your mind.

"And so," common-sense adds, "we are left with no standard of reality. There is no distinction between what I see and what I imagine. The black rat which I see when I am sober, and the pink rat which I think I see when I am drunk, are equally real — or perhaps I should say: equally false. This is absurd."

It is obviously necessary to distinguish between these two types of mental pictures. But instead of calling the pink rat unreal and black rat real, reality should be allowed to both kinds of rat, and a different sort of distinction should be made. It is this: the pink rat does not fit into your mental picture-gallery; it is odd; it is inconsistent with almost every other picture. But the black rat does fit in — its picture not only looks like other rat-pictures in your mind, but moves like them, and sounds like them and is seen against similar pictorial backgrounds.

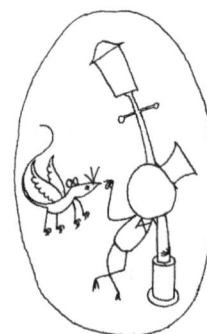

Let us say that both pictures are real, but the first, being out of keeping with the rest of the mental exhibition, is put into your mental lumber-room along with other misfits. That is because you are sane. Lunatics let their lumber-rooms overflow into their picture-galleries.

But you are not a mere accumulation of pictures, put together just anyhow. You are like a busy Art Centre which does infinitely more than collect for collecting's sake.

For example, when a new picture arrives (a picture of an apple, say) the word is passed down to the Art Centre's cellars, and an assortment of pictures to do with apples is rushed up to the ground floor, where they are compared and contrasted with the new picture. Seen along with the others this new picture acquires meaning. It finds its proper place, as an apple, and as a particular sort of apple; eventually it is filed away in the basement for future reference.

Sorting is always going on in the Art Centre. Pictures — some coming from the unknown outside world and others from the largely unexplored basement — are continually being arranged and re-arranged to form interesting sequences or patterns. As part of such patterns they have significance, whereas the pictures taken individually are meaningless.

A curious fact is that the canvases coming in from outside have a tendency to arrive in a certain established order. A picture of a darkening sky is commonly followed by pictures of lighted lamps, of stars, of a spread dinner table, of a game of bridge, and a bed. Then the pictures cease for a little while to come in from outside, and, instead, surrealistic drawings are sent up from the deeper basements, arranged in arbitrary ways, and returned before daybreak.

The Art Centre is not cold-blooded about its work. Some pictures it approves of whole-heartedly, some it dislikes, some it is positively scared of. Naturally it does all it can to encourage the submission of the sort of pictures it likes — pictures of good food, a comfortable home, friends, plenty of money, and so on — and discourage the other sort. It is constantly advertising for the pictures it requires to complete sections of the collection, or to improve their tone...

The parable breaks down, of course. It can give little idea how complex you are. What concerns us here, however, is that you are this picture world; you are these star-pictures and tramcar-pictures and dream-pictures organised, built up into patterns which have meaning and value.

This is more extraordinary the more you think about it. To get an idea of what is involved, try asking yourself where, exactly, you are.

You are not trapped in your bag of molecules, in your cell-city, in your hundred and fifty pounds of flesh and bone. Normally, at any rate, such things do not concern you. You live your life outside that restricted world, in the outer world of stars, trees, tramcars, and men and women. These things, plus millions more like them, are you.

You are myriads of spaceless, weightless, positionless pictures, worked up into a world picture, a grand picture of pictures. Whether you are looking through a telescope at a spiral nebula so far away that it's light takes a million years to jump to your eye, or, through a microscope, at red corpscle in human blood (at some hundreds of millions to the drop), what you see belongs to you, is part of you.

Not even the sky is your limit. All that you see or hear or feel or imagine, is you. To every landscape and seascape and skyscape you can say: 'I am not here, but over there. All these mountains, these waters, these skies, are me!' Try to think of something that is not you, and immediately, by the mere act of thinking of it, you have added it to yourself.

CHAPTER X

THE UNIVERSAL SHOW

We have seen how you spread out till you include, if not the whole world, at least as much of it as your mind can grasp.

In Chapter III, while we were looking at you as a body, we arrived at a somewhat similar conclusion, namely, that you expand by means of your bodily extensions, till your limits are those of the Universe. But in Chapter IV we found that directly you are seen in your social setting, as one little human body amongst 200,000,000 others, we obtain a very different portrait of you. You shrink almost to insignificance. The time has now come to repeat this deflating process, and to see you as one mind in a world of minds.

This time there is a serious difficulty: you know nothing about the 'outside' world. For you there really is no outside world. Either an object exists in your mind, or it does not. If it does, then it is part of you. If it does not, then you cannot know anything about it.

You cannot prove the existence of anything but the ideas in your mind — and they are self-evident. In particular, you cannot prove the existence, outside your mind, of other men's bodies — let alone their minds.

But we have come to a blind-alley, and proceeding along this path, though eminently reasonable, will not get you very far. In any case you have a conviction that your friends and I and the rest of men do exist, and that we know the same world as you do. There is a chance you may be wrong, of course, but it would be odd to have such powerful convictions and yet be absolutely mistaken.

For these reasons (perhaps you can think of others) you will, no doubt, come to the conclusion that you are not alone in the world, and that there are other men in it, and that we are like you.

We decided in the previous chapter that you are the world of sky, stars, tramcars, and all the rest, built up into an extremely complicated picture-system. So am I. So are the rest of men. In these 'outside'

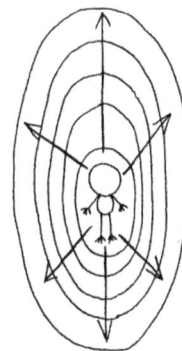

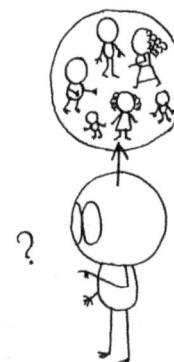

things we all live our lives. There are as many 'Art Centres' as there are men, women, and children, but their pictures are shared.

No doubt your collection, and your arrangement of your collection, are somewhat different from mine and from everybody else's. But an apple-picture, for example, probably means very much the same to me as to you.

Pictures of darkening skies, stars, and lamp-light occur in the same order in my mind and in yours. This book, which is really a picture-pattern in my mind, must correspond to a similar picture-pattern in your mind, otherwise you would have given up reading it long ago.

In other words, your world, though it has a unique twist, is my world. We are built out of the same spaceless picture-material. The fact that my twist is different from yours is one of the things that saves us from being identical, but it does not prevent us from overlapping. You are one angle on the world, and I am a slightly different angle; the world itself is much the same in either case.

Or put it this way: there is a world of 'ideas' capable of being known by us men. It is spaceless and weightless, yet it contains everything that appears to us to belong in space. Now this world is our common property. We all share it; we all belong in it; we are all part of it; but none of us embraces the whole of it. Each is a limited aspect of it.

This means that you and I are not apart. Suppose we are both looking at a distant landscape. The trees, and sky, and clouds, and mountains — all belong to me, are part of me. When you look at them you are looking at me. But they are also part of you. You are looking at both me and yourself.

Out there we intermingle.

Besides you and me, there are something like 2,000 million men, women, and children on the Earth, and none of us live our lives imprisoned in our bodies. We are apparently separate from each other, yet out there, in our world, we become one.

CHAPTER XI

THE CENTRE OF THE PICTURE

"I still have had no answer," says common-sense, "to the question: what is my mind? You have enlarged upon what it is not, but have avoided saying what it is. Pictures that take up no room, and the complicated business of dealing with the pictures — these are only part of the machinery of my mind and not the thing itself, much as bricks and windows and doors are bits of a house, but nothing like the house. What is mind itself, in its essence?

"And that brings me to my second point. I am not a collection of pictures constantly being shuffled in a picture gallery: I am the picture-collector. Who is this collector? Deep down in me, below all the bric-à-brac that goes to make up my mind, I believe there is something — call it what you like — which is the real me. Tell me exactly what I am referring to when I say I. What is it, where did it come from, where is it going?"

First of all, then, what is mind?

In a sense you know very well what mind is, though you are at a loss when it comes to putting your knowledge into words. You know what mind is, because you are a mind. You are a mind all the time, whether you want to be or not, without a moment's rest, and if you have not got inside information on the subject, who has? It is the only thing you know, but for that very reason it is at the same time unknowable. The difficulty is that there is nothing you can compare it with, or use to throw light upon it.

The fact is that the more intimately a thing belongs to you, and the more you are that thing, the more difficult it is for your intelligence to come to grips with it.

To illustrate this point, consider first your body. If you were to lose a leg or an arm, you would still feel that the essential you was intact. Probably you can, without a great deal of effort, imagine yourself as entirely outside your body, yet still remaining yourself. In other

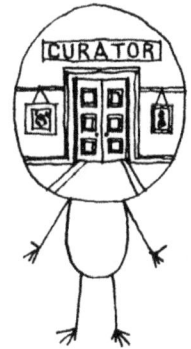

words, your body is not so much you that you cannot mentally get far enough away from it to appreciate something of its nature. You can describe in minute details the way it works, handle it, be sure of it.

Next take your mind. You can imagine yourself deprived of some of your memories, but can you imagine yourself without your mind as a whole? Can you imagine yourself remaining yourself if you forgot all your experiences, or if your mind were a perfect blank from now on? At the very least you will agree that it is far more difficult to think of yourself carrying on minus your mind, than minus your body. Putting it crudely, your mind is more a part of you than your body is. It lies nearer the centre, and you cannot get away from it to take a look at it from a distance. For this reason you can never know the nature of your mind in the same sense as you can know the nature of your body.

And, finally, take this something that common-sense says is the realest you. It lies right at the centre, and obviously you can never get outside it, or amputate a bit of it, or even influence it in any way. There it is, pure, indivisible, simple, unknowable, yet more you than your body, more you than your mind.

Your outer husk, the body, can be seen and heard, can be weighed and have its temperature taken, can be measured and taken to pieces. Your second husk, the mind, can neither be seen nor heard, can neither be weighed nor measured nor located, though it is rich in detail and its functions can be described by means of symbols. And your core, that central something, is not only beyond sight and hearing, but also beyond all description and reason. One of the very few things one can say of it is that it exists, and there are many who profess that they are not even sure of that.

But in the last resort it is meaningless to say that any one part of you is less essential, less really you, than another part. And it is only superficially that body is more knowable than mind, and that mind is more knowable than the ego or self; actually, all three are equally mysterious. It is really as impossible to understand what your body is, as to understand what your mind is, and your mind is no less a mystery than common-sense's 'collector of pictures'. In any case, you are not three, but one.

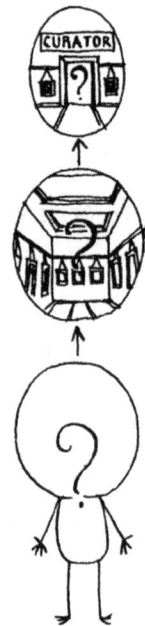

When, like an infant with a clock, we start pulling this unity to pieces to see how it works, we fail utterly. We fail because in trying to understand that unity we divide it, and to divide a unity is to destroy its oneness.

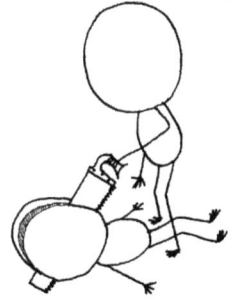

CHAPTER XII

THE COMPOSITE PORTRAIT

For this portrait of yourself we have made eleven preliminary studies. They are no more than lightning sketches. Inevitably they lack detail; inevitably they are distorted; inevitably they are but samples of the innumerable sketches — each drawn from a novel angle — which could be made of you.

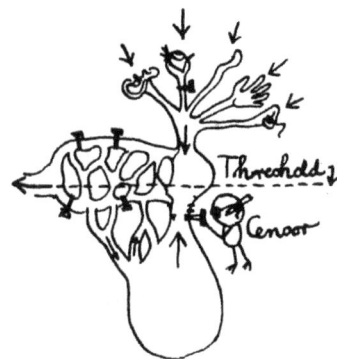

To take three obvious omissions: There is the psycho-analyst's impression of you as a seething mass of primitive and mostly disreputable impulses, which is only kept from boiling over by an elaborate system of safety-valves. There is the physiologist's impression of you as chemical factory, irrigation system, telephone exchange, radio station, and prime-mover, rolled into one. There is the Marxist's impression of you as a drop of water in a mighty social stream that is flowing, circuitously but relentlessly, to a land where each will give according to his ability to each according to his need.

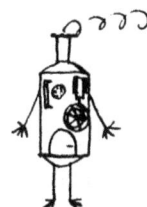

But however many studies we were to make — each having its measure of truth — they would still fall immeasurably short of the whole truth. For you are not a hundred –ologies; you are one. To glimpse you as a whole it would be necessary, not merely to add up all that physics, chemistry, biochemistry, biology, psychology, sociology, and philosophy have to say about you, but to synthesise their findings, to weld them into one grand –ology. Science is very far from such a synthesis. It sees you piecemeal, never as a whole.

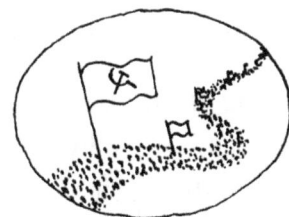

What science has failed to do, we cannot attempt here. It is obviously impossible for us to make a clear composite picture out of our eleven sketches. But perhaps we can trace certain broad lines which are common to each — lines which may hint at the pattern of the whole you.

Throughout this book common-sense has maintained that:

(1) You are limited.

(2) You are separate.

(3) You are knowable.

To which, after some investigation, we replied that:

(1) You are unlimited.

(2) You are unseparate.

(3) You are unknowable.

Or in greater detail:

(1) You are unlimited as a body. You spread out in space, by growing extensions of your skin, arms, legs, digestive apparatus, and sense organs, till your body wraps the Earth. You spread beyond these till you include the plants and animals that make your life possible, and the soil and air and sunlight that make all life possible. In fact, there is no telling where your body ends. It has no limits. (Chapter III)

And you spread back in time, as a gigantic distributed body, some two thousand million years. Ultimately, your past is the whole of events which have helped to make you what you are, and your future is the effect you will go on having on the world. It is impossible to say when you began and when you will end. (Chapter VI)

You are unlimited as a mind. You are all you experience, and your experience is world-wide. You are all your mind is capable of containing, and who can measure your mind's capacity? (Chapter IX)

(2) You are unseparate as a body. You are a minute and insignificant particle which lives and moves and has its being, alongside hundreds of millions like yourself, inside a creature whose body resembles a gigantic creeper. (Chapter IV)

You are an even more insignificant particle inside the body of a vast but scattered living thing, of whom the Earth-creature is a sort of organ. (Chapter VII)

You are unseparate as a mind. Out there, in the world which is you and which is also me, you intermingle with me and with all men. (Chapter X)

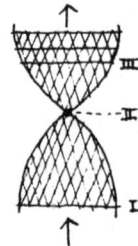

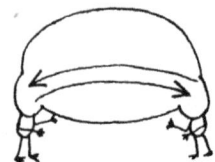

(3) You are unknowable as a body. You are empty space sparsely dotted with utterly mysterious entities. (Chapter VIII) You are a city whose myriads of inhabitants are made of dead material, yet live; and how you, an intelligent and self-conscious being, arise out of the union of these stupid and un-self-conscious inhabitants is beyond all conjecture. (Chapter II) Briefly, you do not know what your raw material is, or how it is worked up into the finished article, or what the finished article is, or how it is maintained. (Chapter V) In any case, if your body has an existence in itself apart from our ideas about it, we cannot know what that existence is like. (Chapter I)

You are unknowable as a mind. You are stuff which is invisible, takes up no room, and is not located anywhere. As for what mind is, the question is unanswerable. (Chapter XI)

These, in barest outline, are the results of our contest with common-sense.

You may agree with these conclusions, yet still have a lingering doubt as to whether it is advisable to inquire too closely into your own nature.

On this subject three things may be said. Firstly, it is true that we do not like our minds to be unsettled, but it is no less true that disturbances are often fruitful — after all, growth is a sort of disturbance, and it is impossible to grow mentally without losing peace of mind now and then. Secondly, the minds of most of us are not particularly tranquil in any case — the world's state, to say nothing of our private difficulties, sees to that. A little extra disturbance, therefore, is no serious matter, and it is perhaps better for our peace of mind to know the worst — or the best. Thirdly, on your death-bed it will be too late to start wondering what your life was about, and I, for one, would be sorry to die without ever having found time to be surprised at my living. Admittedly it is necessary to be busy, but for men to be completely involved all the time in the business of living is to miss half the point of the business. It is awareness far more than activity that distinguishes us from the lower animals. The higher the animal the more it is aware, and the more it is aware the more it truly lives.

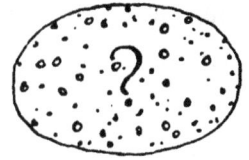

Or you may agree that an attempt at self-knowledge is a duty, and well worth while as an intellectual exercise, yet doubt whether it can be of real value to you, or have an appreciable effect on your life.

The suggestions that follow are more personal, and therefore more controversial, than the rest of this book. In any case they are no more than hints; at least one more book would be needed to do any sort of justice to the many questions — the free-will problem and the problem of evil are instances — that are involved.

Let us take our three main conclusions and try to find out what bearing, if any, they could have on the problem of unhappiness.

(1) You are unlimited.

A sense of limitation is one of the principal causes of human misery. Everyone wants to feel big and important; everyone hates the feeling of being shut in, restricted, small; everyone wants to grow in some sense. There are several things that can be done to satisfy this urge.

For instance, you may expand by adding to yourself great possessions — a magnificent home, gardens, cars, servants. You may accumulate money and invest it all over the world, and extend yourself that way. Or you may achieve fame, popularity, or notoriety, which are ways of making yourself felt at a distance.

All these are means of growth. In so far as your growth falls short of your desires, you are unhappy. Even if you are moderately successful, and grow all the possessions, money, popularity, and fame that you now hope to, there is the likelihood that you will eventually want more. The more you grow the less each new addition satisfies. Another source of unhappiness is that the more you grow the more vulnerable you become. You have more to lose, and it is easier to lose possessions than to acquire them.

Now some moralists would say that these facts only prove how much better it is to rest content with what you are and what you have. I think these moralists are wrong. The urge to expand is deep-rooted in human nature, and the real problem is not how to get rid of the urge but how to satisfy it completely.

Such wealth and fame as come your way should no doubt be enjoyed, but they should be seen as a very limited sort of growth incapable of giving lasting satisfaction. They are insignificant and unworthy extensions of yourself, and it is only a mistaken view of yourself which can make them, in prospect, seem supremely attractive.

For you are already unlimited. As in the song, you can already say that the whole wide world belongs to you. Alongside such property, a bigger house, more acres, a fatter bank balance, and a national reputation, look somewhat trivial. What difference will a few extra belongings make to one who is world-wide? Why should the praise of a few thousand men for a few decades seem so immensely attractive to a creature who has lived in a million men, and was born hundreds of millions of years ago, and is as much of the world as his mind can lay hold of?

Your lack of limits is not a theory. It is a fact. But being a fact which is contrary to common-sense, it is difficult to make your own, so that it becomes part of your everyday thinking. Only constant practice will enable you to realise something of your vastness.

When you hear music and the songs of birds, when you look at pictures and flowers and the faces of your friends, you can truly say: "It is myself that I see and hear. I include all these; they are not outside me. Instead of being trapped in a little body, I am at large out there among these well-known and well-loved things. Mind and body, I am there, spreading towards the whole."

(2) You are unseparate.

Loneliness is another of the causes of our human misery. How often we feel separated from people and from things, abandoned by everybody and everything, intolerably apart. At some time or other, all of us have felt the smart of loneliness; with some it is a permanent feeling.

A great deal of our time is spent in an effort to overcome the sense of being lost in the world. Social functions, games, religious observances, or any other activity in which the individual loses himself in the group, are the means we employ. We are social animals, and sociableness, as we saw in Chapter VIII, is the ground plan on which the Universe is built. When we merge ourselves in human groups we are simply carrying on the process by which our electrons, atoms, molecules, and cells make us possible.

For some of us the group is the family, and conscious membership of it, in an alien and more or less hostile world, gives a sense of security and peace. For others it is a church, a political party, or a nation which commands loyalty and, in return, gives relief from loneliness.

But units like these, considered as wholes in which to merge yourself, have at least three serious defects:

Firstly, they are apt to let you down. You may be unswervingly loyal to your family, yet for many reasons it may force you back into your loneliness. Your church or your political party may overlook both your genuineness and your services and give you the cold shoulder. And nations have a well-known habit of ignoring even their best men, or, worse still, eliminating them. Such unreliability in the objects of your loyalty is bound, from time to time, to make you feel separate from them.

Secondly, they are exclusive. Enthusiastic membership of a family, a political party, a church, or a nation, is apt to remove your sense of apartness in one narrow sphere only to emphasise it in a bigger sphere. Seen from the bosom of your family, the outside world has an artificially hostile look; the party politician is noted for his rancour; the earnestness of the churchman is too often the measure of his narrowness; the nationalist thrives on the real or imagined opposition of foreigners. The price you have to pay for the consolation of losing yourself in such limited groups is the heightened feeling of your separation from the world outside the group. That price is a heavy one. Loyalty to something bigger is needed.

Thirdly, they are not completely satisfying. However attached you may be to your family, to your church, to your nation, or to some other unit, there will still be times when you experience utter loneliness. Your family life touches you at many points, but there are sides of you which have very little to do with it. Rarely, if ever, can a church or a political party command total allegiance; a part of you remains aloof and alone. Your deeper being is untouched by these (surface) loyalties and craves a grander attachment. Even the perfervid nationalist must have moments when he sinfully doubts the worthiness of the group he adores.

These three defects suggest that we should try to find a more trustworthy, a more inclusive, a more satisfying whole, to which you can consciously attach your self.

Is the Earth-creature of Chapter IV such a whole?

Your membership of this creature is no surface matter. Whether you are conscious of your membership or not, whether or not you want to belong to him (or it), makes little difference. For you are inextricably involved. Your body belongs inside his body, and there is no playing truant. As a mind, you are what you are because of your membership in him. In him, you and I and all men become one, irrespective of class, creed, and nation.

Perhaps we have here a whole that satisfies our conditions, one that is truly worthy of our allegiance. And yet, in practice, it is found unworthy. There have been several attempts to set up Man, or something else which roughly (but not exactly) corresponds to our Earth-creature, as an object worthy of human adoration, and all of them have failed. The reason is this: you need to feel that you belong to something bigger, less restrictedly human, more independent of yourself. Awareness of your membership of the Earth-creature is a step in the right direction, but you need to travel further to find a whole big enough to lose yourself in utterly.

What about Life — that ancient creature with a scattered body which still remains one body? Is this whole sufficiently big, sufficiently super-human?

You are as much a part of Life's body as the leaf is part of the tree. No particle of you is outside this body. As a minute 'cell' in it you have communion not with men only, but with all living things.

But once more there are difficulties. What is Life's body but a thin film round a grain of dust that is whirling in an alien Universe? Seen in its world-setting, Life on the Earth is indefinitely tiny, and certainly not big enough to satisfy you. It is also vulnerable — one day life on this planet will probably peter out — and you need to feel that you belong to something that cannot die. And finally, you cannot feel wholly loyal to a creature that is seemingly indifferent to your fate (your death will not inconvenience it), that is full of apparently destructive elements (such as disease germs), and whose mind, if any, is to say the least a doubtful quantity.

Life then, will not suit our purpose. What else is left?

The whole. Conscious membership of the whole, and nothing less than the whole, can satisfy you.

There can be nothing more permanent, vaster, more inclusive, than the whole of things. As a part of it, you are separate from nothing. In it you mingle physically with all things; in it you mingle as a mind with all other minds. In it you are one with all men, one with all that your mind can grasp.

If the whole lets you down, nothing else can save you. But is it possible to think of the whole letting a part of itself down? This is a large question, but whatever the answer, this much may be said: only awareness of your membership of the whole can permanently relieve your loneliness.

(3) You are unknowable.

Anxiety is a third cause of unhappiness. By anxiety I mean worry about what you have been, about what you are, and about what will become of you. You want peace of mind, and that is hard to find.

Almost the only sort of peace that many of us know is the peace of physical and mental exhaustion. Games, hard work, and sexual activity can give it, but the unrest soon returns. Things which 'take you out of yourself' do not keep you absent very long, and the old problem of the restless self, anxious, insecure, without roots, crops up again and again. No amount of hard living, or even hard thinking, can compensate you for the lack of a place of refuge, where you do not need to be taken out of yourself because you have really tackled the question of what you are.

This unrest is the result of a mistaken notion of your own nature. It comes about because you have an overwhelming sense of self-dependence. Ordinarily, you imagine that you are in your own hands, and that you can paddle your own canoe with some success — if you are lucky. But there are dangerous rapids and submerged rocks in the stream, and the navigator's skill is not always up to the mark. Hence the anxiety.

However much appearances belie the fact, you are not self-determining. Your nature is beyond your control. How can you consciously govern depths which are far beyond the reach of consciousness?

There is only one thing to do — surrender. Admit that anxiety about yourself is futile. Say whatever it is that has got you in hand, has really got you in hand. Become acquainted with the amazing fact that you exist, and that you exist without being able really to understand a single item in the whole astounding process. Accept the situation.

But not with a dull, unenthusiastic acceptance. There is a sort of peace, almost indistinguishable from death, which is worse than anxiety. You may be, and you are, unknowable, but you are also wonderful.

Potentially, a thousandth part of what you know about yourself is enough material to fill you with endless surprise. The conviction that your unknowable being is sustained by something immeasurably bigger than yourself can stimulate as well as satisfy. The sort of peace which follows from this conviction need not make you less active. You may be as busy as ever, but back of your activity will lie your mental surrender to the whole. Activity will then be seen for what it is, the whole working through one of its parts.

To sum up, we have found that you are unlimited, unseparate, and unknowable, and that a full realisation of these three facts can overcome your sense of restriction, your loneliness, and your unrest. A man who could always live in the knowledge that he spreads out to embrace the whole, that he is inextricably mixed up with every part of the whole, and that his entire being is sustained by the whole, would have peace, security, and happiness.

Such a state of mind is beyond human reach, but that is no reason for discouragement. Even a little awareness brings its measure of freedom, and there is a sense in which each increase of awareness is its own reward.